BOOK 1 Topics FROM A TO Z

Steps to Success in Listening and Speaking

Irene E. Schoenberg

Longman

Topics from A to Z, Book 1:
Steps to Success in Listening and Speaking

Pearson Education, 10 Bank Street, White Plains, NY 10606

Vice president of multimedia and skills: Sherry Preiss
Executive editor: Laura Le Drean
Development editor: Debbie Sistino
Senior production editor: Robert Ruvo
Director of manufacturing: Patrice Fraccio
Senior manufacturing buyer: Nancy Flaggman
Photo research: Pamela Kohn
Cover design: Stuart Goldstein
Text design: 2AM Diseño
Text composition: 2AM Diseño
Text font: 11/14 Times Roman
Illustrations: Luis Briseño / 2AM Diseño

Photo Credits: **page ix** (left) © 1998 PhotoDisc, Inc. All rights reserved.; (right) © 1998 PhotoDisc, Inc. All rights reserved.; **page 2** (top) © Tammie Arroyo/Getty Images; (bottom center left) © Royalty-Free/Corbis; (bottom right) © Rufus F. Folkks/Corbis; **page 3** (left) © 1998 PhotoDisc, Inc. All rights reserved.; (right) © 2004 Hemera Technologies Inc. All rights reserved; **page 5** (top) © Dan Herrick/ZUMA/Corbis; (middle left) © Photofest (212) 633-6330; (middle right) © Warner Bros/The Kobal Collection; (bottom) © Photofest (212) 633-6330; **page 7** (left) © 1998 PhotoDisc, Inc. All rights reserved.; (right) © 1998 PhotoDisc, Inc. All rights reserved.; **page 11** (left) © 1998 PhotoDisc, Inc. All rights reserved.; **page 13** (middle) © Royalty-Free/Corbis; (bottom) © FoodPix; **page 14** (bottom left) © Shaun Egan/Stone; (bottom center) Julio Cueva, Sheila Michael, Julie Schmidt; (bottom right) © The Image Bank; **page 15** (bottom left) © 2004 Hemera Technologies Inc. All rights reserved; (bottom right) © 1998 PhotoDisc, Inc. All rights reserved.; **page 16** National Museum of Natural History © 2004 Smithsonian Institution; **page 17** (top) © Harald Sund/Getty Images; (middle) © Tim Graham/Corbis; (bottom) © Free Agents Limited/Corbis; **page 18** (bottom left) © Lester Lefkowitz/Corbis; (bottom center) © Digital Vision; (bottom right) © Grant Smith/Corbis; **page 19** (bottom right) © Digital Vision Ltd.-All rights reserved.; **page 21** (top) © Digital Vision; **page 23** (bottom left) © 1998 PhotoDisc, Inc. All rights reserved.; (bottom right) © 1998 PhotoDisc, Inc. All rights reserved.; **page 27** (right) © 1998 PhotoDisc, Inc. All rights reserved.; **page 30** (Mark McGrath left) © Evan Agostini/Getty Images; (Mark McGrath right) © Evan Agostini/Getty Images; (Halle Berry left) © Dave Hogan/ Getty Images; (Halle Berry right) © Kurt Vinion/Getty Images; (Serena Williams left) © Eric Ryan/Getty Images; (Serena Williams right) © Stephen Sugarman/Getty Images Entertainment; (bottom left) © Michael T. Sedam/ Corbis; (bottom center left) © Lenny Furman/Getty Images Entertainment; (bottom center right) © Bettmann/Corbis; (bottom right) © Hulton-Deutsch Collection/Corbis; **page 31** (left) © 1998 PhotoDisc, Inc. All rights reserved.; (right) © 1998 PhotoDisc, Inc. All rights reserved.; **page 32** (left) © Ryan McVay/Getty Images; (center left) © Michael Prince/Corbis; (center right) © David Sacks/Getty Images; (right) © Michael Prince/Corbis; **page 33** © Hulton-Deutsch Collection/Corbis; **page 34** (top) © Peter Grant; (bottom left) © W. Geiersperger/Corbis; (bottom center left) © Jack Andersen/FoodPix;

(continued on page xi)

Library of Congress Cataloging-in-Publication Data

Schoenberg, Irene, 1946–
    Topics from A–Z. Book 1 / Irene Schoenberg
        p. cm.
    ISBN 0-13-185073-3 (alk. paper)
  1. English language—Textbooks for foreign speakers. 2. English language--Spoken English--Problems, exercises, etc. 3. Conversation--Problems, exercises, etc. 4. Listening--Problems, exercises, etc. I. Title.
PE1128.S3458 2005
428.3'4--dc22

                                                          2005040795

ISBN: 0-13-185073-3

Printed in the United States of America
3 4 5 6 7 8 9 10 VHJ 09 08 07 06 05

Contents

Unit 1   Actors   2

Unit 2   Books   6

Unit 3   Chocolate   10

Unit 4   Diamonds and Other Jewelry   14

Unit 5   Emergencies and Disasters   18

Unit 6   Fables and Fairy Tales   22

Unit 7   Gestures   26

Unit 8   Hairstyles   30

Unit 9   Ice   34

Unit 10   Junk and Garbage   38

Unit 11   Kandinsky, Klee, and Modern Art   42

Unit 12   Laughter   46

Unit 13   Masks   50

Unit 14   Names, Nicknames, and Titles   54

Unit 15   Ounces and Other Measurements   58

Unit 16   Photography   62

Unit 17   Queens   66

Unit 18   "Red" Idioms   70

Unit 19   Strange and Unusual Things   74

Unit 20   Tai Chi and Other Martial Arts   78

Unit 21   Uncles   82

Unit 22   Vending Machines   86

Unit 23   Weddings   90

Unit 24 $X + Y = ?$ 94

Unit 25   Yen, Peso, and Other Currencies   98

Unit 26   Zoos   102

Tapescript   109

Scope and Sequence

Unit	Title	Functions	
1 Page 2	Actors	Expressing opinions about actors and acting	
2 Page 6	Books	Talking about book preferences; Comparing books and computers	
3 Page 10	Chocolate	Discussing chocolate eating habits	
4 Page 14	Diamonds and Other Jewelry	Expressing attitudes toward diamonds; Talking about jewelry preferences	
5 Page 18	Emergencies and Disasters	Telling about disasters and emergencies; Sharing opinions about disaster movies	
6 Page 22	Fables and Fairy Tales	Talking about favorite fairy tales; Expressing opinions about scary stories	
7 Page 26	Gestures	Guessing gestures; Comparing body language of men and women	
8 Page 30	Hairstyles	Talking about haircuts; Describing different types of hairstyles	
9 Page 34	Ice	Telling what winter sports you like; Expressing opinions about weather and work	
10 Page 38	Junk and Garbage	Talking about throwing things away; Expressing opinions about flea markets	
11 Page 42	Kandinsky, Klee, and Modern Art	Talking about preferences in art; Expressing opinions about art and beauty	
12 Page 46	Laughter	Telling about things that make you laugh; Expressing opinions about laughter as medicine	
13 Page 50	Masks	Describing masks; Giving opinions about costume parties	

Listening	Conversation Practice	Check This Out
1. Trying Out for a Play 2. Facts about Antonio Banderas	Sharing information and opinions about acting and actors; Buying movie tickets	Famous Actors
1. Where People Get Books 2. J.K. Rowling and Harry Potter	Buying a book at a bookstore	Books as Gifts
1. Chocolate and Health 2. Ganache: A Type of Chocolate	Giving and accepting a gift	Foods with Chocolate; Word Game
1. How Experts Judge Diamonds 2. The Hope Diamond	Information Gap: Stones and metals	The Crown Jewels and the Tower of London
1. A Blackout 2. Forest Fires in Canada	Discussing what to do in an emergency	Warning Signs
1. Hans Christian Andersen's "The Ugly Duckling" 2. Aesop's Fable- "Sour Grapes"	Story: The Miser	Maurice Sendak Illustration
1. A Universal Gesture 2. Customs in Brazil	Learning body parts and Describing gestures	American Gestures
1. An Appointment at the Hair Salon 2. Wigs in Great Britain	Talking about preferences in men's hairstyles	Unusual Hairstyles for Women
1. Ice Sculptures 2. The Inuit of Canada	Using ice breakers	Building an Igloo
1. Space Junk 2. Throwing Away Something Valuable	Discussing ideas from environmentalists	How Workers Save Things
1. Similarities between Kandinsky and Klee 2. How to Understand Art	Discussing how much a painting is worth	Kandinsky Painting: *Contrasting Sounds*
1. What Makes People Laugh 2. Why It's Good to Laugh	Giving the end to a story-reading a story aloud	Different Ways People Laugh
1. Masks in Venice 2. A Mask from Burkino Faso	Describing masks and costumes	Yup'ik Masks

Scope and Sequence

Unit	Title	Functions	
14 Page 54	Names, Nicknames, and Titles	Discussing names and nicknames; Expressing opinions about remembering names	
15 Page 58	Ounces and Other Measurements	Asking and answering questions about using measurements; Giving an opinion about a measurement system	
16 Page 62	Photography	Talking about photos; Expressing opinions about photos at parties	
17 Page 66	Queens	Exchanging information and expressing opinions about royalty	
18 Page 70	"Red" Idioms	Talking about the color red; Expressing opinions about teens and the color red	
19 Page 74	Strange and Unusual Things	Describing a strange event; Expressing opinions about unusual food	
20 Page 78	Tai Chi and Other Martial Arts	Telling how you relax; Expressing preferences about watching sports	
21 Page 82	Uncles	Describing uncles; Expressing opinions about relatives and friends	
22 Page 86	Vending Machines	Talking about vending machine purchases; Expressing opinions about food from vending machines	
23 Page 90	Weddings	Describing wedding preferences, traditions, and gifts; Expressing opinions about marriage and family	
24 Page 94	X + Y = ?	Discussing puzzle preferences; Giving opinions about the value of puzzles	
25 Page 98	Yen, Peso, and Other Currencies	Describing coins; Expressing opinions about money and happiness	
26 Page 102	Zoos	Describing a pet; Discussing sayings about animals	

Listening	Conversation Practice	Check This Out
1. Quiz Show: The Name Game 2. Naming Babies in Germany	Choosing nicknames	Puzzle: Find the Names
1. Prefixes 2. Quiz Show: Ask Any Question	Guessing distances and weights	Common Measurements
1. The Life of Alfred Steiglitz 2. Conversation about a Photo	Talking about a photo you took	Photograph by Brett Weston
1. Queen Liliuokalani 2. The Queen Mary 2	Telling a fairy tale	Palaces around the World
1. The origin of the idiom, "cut through the red tape" 2. Psychology of the Colors *Red* and *Blue*	Creating situations with "red"	Idioms and Colors
1. Unusual Laws 2. Stories from the *Guinness Book of World Records*	Talking about medical surprises	Life on other Planets: E.T.
1. A Radio Ad for Tai Chi 2. Telephone Conversation about Tai Chi Classes	Teaching classmates a martial arts or dance step	Yin and Yang
1. A Description of Relatives 2. "I'll be a monkey's uncle."	Telling about a special relative	Cartoon: Large Families
1. Unusual Things from Vending Machines 2. Cell Phones in South Korea	Discussing the future of vending machines	Out of Order Vending Machine
1. A Wedding Custom in Thailand 2. A Bridal Shower Invitation	Describing a wedding	Cartoon: Why People Marry
1. Children's Riddles 2. A Puzzle: The Weight of Five Dogs	Information Gap: Riddles	A Match Puzzle
1. Changing Money at an Airport 2. A Coin Collector	Matching currency and countries; Describing a bill	Cartoon: Time Traveller's Cheques
1. The History of Zoos 2. Facts about Zoos	GAMES: Animal Alphabet; Guess the Animal	Poster: Balance in Life

Preface

Topics from A-Z, Book 1 is the first of a conversation/listening series written for beginning to low-intermediate level adult and young adult students. Each text contains 26 four-page units, one for each letter of the alphabet. Each unit in Book 1 consists of Facts, Talk about Your Experience, Give Your Opinion, Listening Comprehension 1 and 2, Conversation Practice, and Check This Out. Authentic art and photographs help to maintain student interest throughout the text.

Opening Art

Each unit starts with an engaging piece of art and an accompanying question that get students involved in the unit's content. For example, in Unit 1, "Actors," students look at an illustration of Jennifer Lopez as a teenager and read clues to try to guess who she is. In Unit 8, "Hairstyles," students see illustrations of "before" and "after" hairstyles and give their preferences.

Facts

In this section, groups of students work together trying to answer five or six multiple choice or true/false questions. Illustrations help students understand new words. Some questions are language-based, aiming to increase students' knowledge of words and phrases. Others are fun facts about the context. For example, Unit 1, "Actors," includes these questions:

Were you right?

1. Comedies are _____. _____

   a. funny   b. sad   c. serious

2. A _____ makes movies. _____

   a. direction   b. director   c. directory

3. The main actor is the _____. _____

   a. moon   b. sun   c. star

Next, students listen to the facts and compare them to their guesses. Finally, students read the facts aloud and try to remember them. Some will remember all the facts; others will remember only one or two. In time students discover their own learning style. Some write the sentences or take notes. Others read them several times. Some work alone. Others prefer to work with a partner.

Language experts generally agree that students learn best when they focus on, repeat, and try to remember an item. Memory is thus a key to language improvement. In this section, students develop their skills at memorizing interesting and helpful content.

Talk about Your Experience

In this part, students work with a partner to give personal answers to a set of guided questions. Even the most reticent student can participate in this activity. For example, in Unit 6, "Fables and Fairy Tales," students ask each other the following:

	YOU	YOUR PARTNER
• What's your favorite fairy tale or fable? What is it about?		
• Did a story ever scare you? What was it about?		
• Do you like to read to children? Why or why not?		
• Do you like to write your own stories?		

After students have spoken with a partner, a class discussion or a survey gets students to talk to a larger group. The language is controlled, the topics are non-threatening, and the result is that the whole class becomes involved. For example, in Unit 6, students find three classmates who know the same fable, fairy tale, or children's story. Then they write as much as they can about it. Afterwards students read their work to the class.

Give Your Opinion

This section helps students learn how to politely agree or disagree with someone in English. Students hear opinions on tape. A box to the side shows responses, such as: "I think so, too," or "I don't think so." For example, in Unit 6, students hear and respond to the following opinions:

Most fairy tales are too scary for young children.

I think that's true. I remember crying and worrying after I heard the story of *Hansel and Gretel*.

I don't agree. I think children love fairy tales with scary parts.

Responses
I think that's true.
I don't agree.

Students are given an example and encouraged to add their own ideas. In supporting their opinions, students develop critical thinking skills.

Listening Comprehension 1 and 2

These sections include a variety of listening activities. In some, students supply missing words or phrases. In some, they indicate comprehension, and in some, they do tasks based on the listening.

The content is practical and interesting. For example, students hear radio programs, telephone conversations, and "fun facts" stories. Again, the level of the language is controlled, though the content is geared to adults and young adults.

Conversation Practice

In this part, a variety of activities help students improve their conversation skills. For example, in the unit about Queens, students study several vocabulary words, then work with a partner to use the words in a story. In the unit on Martial Arts, students teach a group of classmates a martial arts or dance step, or lead them in a type of exercise. In the unit on Diamonds, students do an Information Gap in which they find out where various gems and metals are from. Some units provide students with social language (functions) that they practice in conversations. In other units, there is a focus on new vocabulary, while others get students to discuss something they had previously heard or read.

Check This Out

A final piece of art — a cartoon, an advertisement, a puzzle, a painting — in combination with a short task, gets students motivated once again to consider and talk about another aspect of the topic.

Acknowledgments

Students are the final arbiters of the value of a text. I thank my students at the International English Language Institute, Hunter College, CUNY, both for their helpful comments and for their enthusiastic reaction to the materials in *Topics from A to Z*.

Publishers are the ones who decide whether or not to use their resources to develop and produce a book. My thanks to all the people at Pearson Education who supported the concept of this series and helped bring it to fruition:

To Joanne Dresner, President of Pearson North America, who listened to my initial ideas for *Topics from A to Z*, and encouraged me to develop them; Sherry Preiss and Laura Le Drean who offered many specific and valuable ways to improve the book and who were so supportive throughout; Robert Ruvo who diligently guided the book through production; Pamela Kohn for her outstanding photo research; John Barnes for his many helpful suggestions; and to my editor Debbie Sistino for her suggestions, overseeing the art and photo research, and helping to obtain many of the beautiful pieces of art that appear in the book. As always, my special thanks to my family—to Harris, Dan, and Dahlia for their love, support, and interest in my work.

Photo Credits

(continued from page ii)
(bottom center right) © Peter Johnson/Corbis; (bottom right) © Stuart Westmorland/Getty Images; **page 35** (left) © 2004 Hemera Technologies Inc. All rights reserved.; (right) © Digital Vision Ltd.-All rights reserved.; **page 36** © The Image Works; **page 38** (bottom left) Ilhan Ramic, Sheila Michael, Julie Schmidt; (bottom center left) © Royalty-Free/Corbis; (bottom center right) © C Squared Studios/Getty Images; (bottom right) © Rob Goldman/Getty Images; **page 39** (right) © 2004 Hemera Technologies Inc. All rights reserved.; **page 40** © Kennedy Space Center; **page 42** (top) © 2004 Artists Rights Society (ARS), New York/VG Bild-Kunst, Bonn and Erich Lessing/Art Resource, NY; (bottom left) © 2004 Artists Rights Society (ARS), New York/ADAGP, Paris and Bridgeman-Giraudon/Art Resource, NY; (bottom right) © 2004 Artists Rights Society (ARS), New York/VG Bild-Kunst, Bonn and Tate Gallery, London/Art Resource, NY; **page 43** (right) © Digital Vision Ltd.-All rights reserved.; **page 45** © 2004 Artists Rights Society (ARS), New York/ADAGP, Paris and Réunion des Musées Nationaux/Art Resource, NY; **page 47** (left) © 1998 PhotoDisc, Inc. All rights reserved.; (right) © 1998 PhotoDisc, Inc. All rights reserved.; **page 49** (left) © James Darell/Getty Images; (right) © Royalty-Free/Corbis; **page 50** (a) © Royalty-Free/Corbis; (b) © Jeremy Horner/Corbis; (c) © Paul Almasy/Corbis; (d) © Bohemian Nomad Picturemakers/Corbis; (bottom left) © Royalty-Free/Corbis; (bottom center left) © Roger Wright/Getty Images; (bottom center right) © Susan Bishop; Papilio/Corbis; (bottom right) © Keren Su/Corbis; **page 51** (left) © 2004 Hemera Technologies Inc. All rights reserved.; (right) © 1998 PhotoDisc, Inc. All rights reserved.; **page 52** © Rolf Bruderer/Corbis; **page 53** (top) African, Burkinabe (Burkina Faso), Nuna peoples. Swooping Hawk Mask. Wood, pigment, 52 inches. Gift of Robert S. Zigler. 1992.9.1. Collection University of Virginia Art Museum.; (bottom) Photograph courtesy of the Smithsonian National Museum of Natural History.; **page 54** (Hideki Matsui) © Joe Skipper/Reuters/Corbis; (Gustavo Kuerten) © Duomo/Corbis; (Shaquille O'Neal) © Lenny Furman/Getty Images Entertainment; (Earvin Johnson) © David Guilburt/Corbis; (bottom left) © Frare/Davis Photography/Brand X Pictures; (bottom center) © Matthias Tunger/Digital Vision; **page 55** (left) © 1998 PhotoDisc, Inc. All rights reserved.; **page 56** © Antonio Luiz Hamdan/Getty Images; **page 59** (left) © 2004 Hemera Technologies Inc. All rights reserved.; (right) © 1998 PhotoDisc, Inc. All rights reserved.; **page 61** (bottom) © W. Geiersperger/Corbis; **page 62** (top) © Lee Gallery. Winchester, MA.; (bottom left) © George Shelley/Corbis; (bottom center left) © Hulton-Deutsch Collection/Corbis; (bottom center right) © Carols Cazalis/Corbis; (bottom right) © Cooperphoto, Inc./Corbis; **page 63** (right) © 1998 PhotoDisc, Inc. All rights reserved.; page 64 (top left) © Digital Vision/Getty Images; (top right) © Scott T. Baxter/Getty Images; (bottom left) © Royalty-Free/Corbis; (bottom right) © Jonelle Weaver/Getty Images; **page 65** (bottom) © The Brett Weston Archive/Corbis; **page 66** (top) © Collection/Getty Images; (bottom left) © Gianni Dagli Orti/Corbis; (bottom center left) © Bettmann/Corbis; (bottom center right) © Ralph A. Clevenger/Corbis; (bottom right) © Royalty-Free/Corbis; **page 67** (left) © 1998 PhotoDisc, Inc. All rights reserved.; (right) © 2004 Hemera Technologies Inc. All rights reserved.; **page 68** © Corbis; **page 69** (top) © Neil Rabinowitz/Corbis; (a) © Jack Fields/Corbis; (b) © Roger Antrobus/Corbis; (c) © Royalty-Free/Corbis; (d) © Charles O'Rear/Corbis; **page 71** (left) © 1998 PhotoDisc, Inc. All rights reserved.; (right) © Digital Vision Ltd.- All rights reserved.; **page 74** (top) © 1989 Roger Ressmeyer/NASA/Corbis; **page 75** (right) © 2004 Hemera Technologies Inc. All rights reserved.; **page 77** © Universal/The Kobal Collection; **page 78** (hapkido) © Marc Asnin/Corbis SABA; (capoeira) © Peter Poby/Corbis; (tai chi) © Jim Arbogast/Corbis; (karate) © Royalty-Free/Corbis; (bottom left) © Reuters/Corbis; (bottom center left) Ryan McVay/Getty Images; (bottom center right) © Peter LaMastro/Getty Images; (bottom right) © Duomo/Corbis **page 79** (left) © 1998 PhotoDisc, Inc. All rights reserved.; (right) © 1998 PhotoDisc, Inc. All rights reserved.; **page 83** (right) © 1998 PhotoDisc, Inc. All rights reserved.; **page 86** (top) © Michael S. Yamashita/Corbis; (bottom left) © Lake County Museum/Corbis; (bottom center) © Bettmann/Corbis; (bottom right) © Royalty-Free/Corbis; **page 87** (left) © 2004 Hemera Technologies Inc. All rights reserved.; (right) © Digital Vision Ltd.-All rights reserved.; **page 89** Ilhan Ramic; **page 90** (top left) © Richard T. Nowitz/Corbis; (top center) © Kersin Geier; Gallo Images/Corbis; (top right) © Lindsay Hebberd/Corbis; **page 91** (left) © 1998 PhotoDisc, Inc. All rights reserved.; (right) © 2004 Hemera Technologies Inc. All rights reserved.; **page 94** (left) © Matthias Kulka/Corbis; (center) © Royalty-Free/Corbis; **page 95** (right) © 1998 PhotoDisc, Inc. All rights reserved.; **page 99** (left) © 1998 PhotoDisc, Inc. All rights reserved.; (right) © 1998 PhotoDisc, Inc. All rights reserved.; **page 102** (bottom left) © Reuters/Corbis; (bottom center) Columbia/The Kobal Collection; (bottom right) © Paul A. Souders/Corbis; **page 103** (top) © Werner H. Müller/Corbis; (bottom right) © 1998 PhotoDisc, Inc. All rights reserved.; **page 105** © Maurice Ambler/Getty Images.

Look at the picture.

- *She is an actor from New York.*
- *Her family is from Puerto Rico.*
- *She was in the movies* Selena, The Wedding Planner, *and* Maid in Manhattan.
- *People call her J.Lo.*

Who is she?

(Check your answer on page 107.)

Facts

A. GROUPS Try to complete the sentences.

Were you right?

1. Comedies are _____.

    a. funny   b. sad   c. serious

    _____

2. A _____ makes movies.

    a. direction   b. director   c. directory

    _____

3. The main actor is the _____.

    a. moon   b. sun   c. star

    _____

4. Many movies are made in _____.

    a. Hollywood   b. Dallas   c. Detroit

    _____

5. Before a play, you say to an actor, "Break _____." It means good luck.

    a. a leg   b. an arm   c. a tooth

    _____

 Now listen and check your answers.

B. GROUPS

- Take turns saying the facts. Then close your books.
- How many facts can you remember? Say all the facts you remember.

Talk about Your Experience

A. PAIRS Answer the questions. Then ask your partner. Add information.

Example: A: *Were you ever in a school play?*

   B: *Yes. I was in many plays in high school. Once I was the king in the play* King Lear. *What about you?*

	YOU	YOUR PARTNER
• Were you ever in a school play?		
• Do you like to act? Did you ever want to be an actor?		
• Do you have a favorite actor? Who?		
• Do you prefer to watch movies at a theater or at home?		

Tell the class about your partner.

Example: *Pierre was a lion in a school play. He doesn't like to act, but he loves to see movies and plays. His favorite actor is Robert DeNiro. He prefers to watch movies at home.*

B. WHOLE CLASS Survey four students.

Ask: How many movies did you see last month?

Report the results to the class.

Example: *Juan saw ten movies. Haruko saw five. Eva saw two. Helena saw one.*

Give Your Opinion

A. Listen to the opinion. Then listen to the responses.

Actors have a great life.

I agree.
They're rich and famous.

I disagree.
It's hard to be an actor.
Most actors are not rich or famous.

B. PAIRS Do you agree with the man or the woman? Add your opinion.

Example: A: *I agree with the woman. Acting is very difficult work.*
   You need to be talented and lucky.

   B: *I disagree . . .*

Responses
I agree.
I disagree.

Two actors want to be in a new play called *Jen*.
Listen and mark the statements true (T) or false (F). Change the false statements to true ones.

_____ 1. The man and woman want to be in the play.

_____ 2. The woman will take any part in the play.

_____ 3. The man will take any part in the play.

_____ 4. The woman read about the play in *The Actor's Newspaper*.

_____ 5. The woman heard about the play from her uncle.

_____ 6. The woman's dad is an actor in the play.

Conversation Practice

A. PAIRS Look at the picture. Complete the conversation. Use the questions in the box.

Can I have two tickets, please?	What time is the next show?
Who's in it?	What kind of a movie is *The Mask of Zorro*?

1. A: _____

   B: It's an action film.

2. A: _____

   B: The next show is at 7:00 p.m.

3. A: _____

   B: Antonio Banderas.

4. A: _____

   B: That'll be $14.00.

B. **PAIRS** Listen to the conversation and check your work. Then practice the conversation with a partner.

C. INFORMATION GAP

Student A, turn to page 106. Student B, turn to page 108.

Warm up: What do you know about Antonio Banderas?

🎧 **Listen to the questions and answers about the actor Antonio Banderas. Then complete the chart.**

Name	
Real Name	
Date of Birth	
Place of Birth	
Number of Brothers and Sisters	
Wife	

Check This Out

GROUPS Do you know these actors? Read the lines to your group. Pretend you are an actor.

"To be or not to be. That is the question."
Hamlet, Sir Laurence Olivier

"Play it Sam."
Casablanca, Humphrey Bogart

"Show me the money."
Jerry Maguire, Cuba Gooding Jr.

How do you choose a book?

the title and cover

the author

an ad

It's a great book!

a friend

Facts

A. GROUPS Guess which statements are true (T) and which statements are false (F).

<u>Your answer</u>

<u>Were you right?</u>

_____ 1. You buy books at a library.

_____

_____ 2. A "bestseller" is a book about selling.

_____

_____ 3. There are paperback and hardcover books.

_____

_____ 4. Agatha Christie's books sold over 2 billion copies.

_____

_____ 5. A "whodunit" is a mystery.

_____

Now listen and check your answers. Change the false statements to true ones.

B. GROUPS

• Take turns saying the facts. Then close your books.
• How many facts can you remember? Say all the facts you remember.

Talk about Your Experience

A. PAIRS Answer the questions. Then ask your partner. Add information.

> **Example:** A: *Did you read a lot as a child?*
> B: *Yes. I loved to read. My favorite book was* Momotaro.

	YOU	YOUR PARTNER

• Did you read a lot as a child?
 	
• What was your favorite book?
 	
• What do you like to read now?
   • books
   • newspapers
   • magazines
   • other
• What kinds of books do you read?
   • novels
   • comic books
   • science fiction
   • history
   • other		

Tell the class about your partner.

> **Example:** *My partner didn't read a lot as a child, but now he does.*

B. WHOLE CLASS Survey four students.

Ask:

Do you read for school, for work, or for fun?

How many books did you read last month?

What kind of books did you read?

Report the results to the class.

> **Example:** *Emiko reads for fun. Last month she read six books. They were all comic books.*

Give Your Opinion

A. 🎧 Listen to the opinion. Then listen to the responses.

> **Computers are more fun than books.**

> I agree.
> You can read and do other things on computers.

> I disagree.
> I like to use computers, but I love to read books.

B. PAIRS Do you agree with the man or the woman? Add your opinion.

> **Example:** A: *I think the woman is right. Computers are more fun than books. I play games, write e-mail messages, write instant messages, and read on my computer.*
> B: *I disagree . . .*

Responses
I agree.
I disagree.

Warm up: Where do you usually get books: at a library, at a bookstore, or from friends?

🎧 **PAIRS** Miki Rice is a student. She is interviewing people about how they get books. Listen to the interview. Then complete the chart.

	Where they get their books
First Man	
Second Man	
First Woman	
Second Woman	

Conversation Practice

A. PAIRS Look at the picture. Complete the conversation. Use the sentences in the box.

> Who's the author?
>
> It's called, *Smart People Like Chocolate*.
>
> We have one copy. It's on that shelf.
>
> Yes, thank you. I'm looking for a book about chocolate.

1. Salesperson: May I help you?

   Customer: _____

2. Salesperson: What's the name of the book?

   Customer: _____

3. Salesperson: _____

   Customer: It's by Coco Bean.

4. Salesperson: Let me check the computer . . . _____

   Customer: Thanks.

B. 🎧 **PAIRS** Listen to the conversation and check your work. Then practice the conversation with a partner.

Warm up: What do you know about Harry Potter? Why are Harry Potter books so popular?

Listen to a talk about J.K. Rowling's books about Harry Potter. Then complete the sentences.

1. You can buy Harry Potter books in _____ countries.

2. Harry Potter books are published in _____ languages.

3. Barnes & Noble bookstores sold _____ million copies of the fifth Harry Potter book in forty-eight hours.

4. One bookseller says, "Harry Potter books have something for everyone—a good _____, a lot of _____, and a fight in which the _____ win."

Check This Out

GROUPS Is a book a good gift?

Give a book. It's a gift you can open again and again.

Unit 3 Chocolate

Some scientists say: Eating chocolate produces the same feeling as falling in love.

What do you think?

Facts

A. GROUPS Try to complete the sentences.

Were you right?

1. The Maya made chocolate _____ years ago.

   a. 700   b. 800   c. 1,700

   _____

2. The Aztecs used cocoa beans for _____.

   a. clothes   b. money   c. homes

   _____

3. The Aztecs put _____ in their chocolate drink.

   a. sugar   b. chilies   c. milk

   _____

4. The _____ introduced chocolate to the rest of Europe.

   a. Dutch   b. English   c. Spanish

   _____

5. The average American eats about _____ pounds of chocolate a year.

   a. twelve   b. ten   c. three

   _____

Now listen and check your answers.

B. GROUPS

• Take turns saying the facts. Then close your books.
• How many facts can you remember? Say all the facts you remember.

A. PAIRS Answer the questions. Then ask your partner. Add information.

Example: A: *Do you like chocolate?*
B: *Yes, I do. It's my favorite candy. What about you?*
A: *I do, too. I eat chocolate every day.*

	YOU	YOUR PARTNER
• Do you like chocolate?		
• How often do you eat chocolate?		
• When was the last time you ate chocolate?		
• Do you drink hot chocolate?		
• Do you give chocolate as a gift? Who do you give it to?		

Tell the class one thing about yourself and one thing about your partner.
Example: *I drink hot chocolate, but Maria doesn't.*

B. WHOLE CLASS Survey four students.
"Comfort foods" make you feel good. For some people, chocolate is a comfort food.
Ask: Do you have any comfort foods? If so, what are they?

Report the results to the class.
Example: *Soup is Sachiko's comfort food. Marco's comfort food is ice cream.*

Give Your Opinion

A. Listen to the opinion. Then listen to the responses.

It's hard to eat only *one* piece of chocolate.

I think so, too.
Chocolate is delicious.
I never eat one piece.
I eat five or six.

I don't think so.
I buy a box of chocolate and
I eat one piece every day.

B. PAIRS Do you agree with the man or the woman? Add your opinion.
Example: A: *I agree with the man. One piece is never enough for me.*
B: *I think so, too . . .*

Responses
I think so, too.
I don't think so.

Listen to a conversation about chocolate and your health. Then answer the questions.

1. What did a study about chocolate show?
2. Where was the study done?
3. How many people were in the study?
4. What's the problem with the study?

Conversation Practice

A. PAIRS Look at the pictures. Complete the conversation. Use the sentences in the box.

OK. Let's.	Mmm. You're right. It is good.	Thanks.
I'm glad.	Sure. Go right ahead.	

1. A: Hi.

   B: Here, this is for you.

   A: _____

2. A: OK if I open it?

   B: _____

3. A: Thanks so much. I love chocolate.

   B: _____

4. A: Let's try some.

   B: _____

5. A: Mmm. It's delicious.

   B: _____

B. **PAIRS** Listen and check your work. Then have a conversation with your partner. Take turns. Pretend to give your partner a gift. Thank your partner for his or her gift.

Warm up: What kind of chocolate do you like best?

chocolate with nuts

milk chocolate

chocolate with fruit

dark chocolate

 Listen to a talk about how one type of chocolate got its name. Then change these false statements to true ones.

1. Ganache is chocolate with nuts.
2. The name "ganache" comes from an Italian word.
3. The worker put milk in some chocolate.
4. A worker was angry and called his boss "stupid."
5. The name "ganache" means "smart person."

Check This Out

A. GROUPS List all the foods that you can make with chocolate.

<u>**FOODS**</u>

chocolate mousse cake

chocolate mousse cake

B. GROUPS List all the words you can make with the letters in *chocolate*.

<u>**C H O C O L A T E**</u>

hat
catch

chocolate-covered strawberries

The group with the most correct foods and words wins.

Diamonds and Other Jewelry

What is your birthstone?

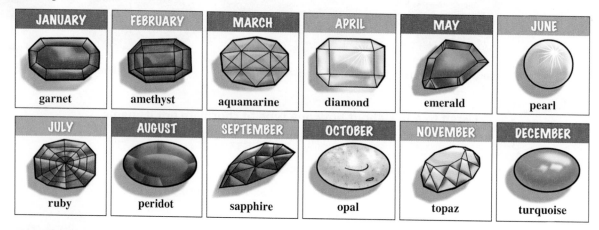

JANUARY	FEBRUARY	MARCH	APRIL	MAY	JUNE
garnet	amethyst	aquamarine	diamond	emerald	pearl

JULY	AUGUST	SEPTEMBER	OCTOBER	NOVEMBER	DECEMBER
ruby	peridot	sapphire	opal	topaz	turquoise

Facts

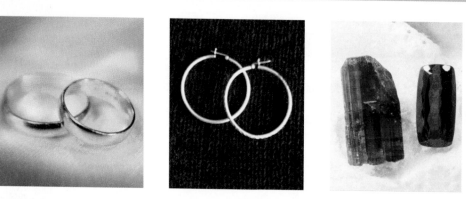

A. GROUPS Guess which statements are true (T) and which statements are false (F).

Your answer		Were you right?

_____ 1. Until the mid-1700s, most diamonds came from Thailand. _____

_____ 2. The biggest diamond in the world is the Star of Alaska. _____

_____ 3. We measure diamonds in carats. _____

_____ 4. Most diamonds are about 3 million years old. _____

_____ 5. Emeralds are the hardest stones. _____

_____ 6. Gold and silver are metals. Diamonds and emeralds are stones. _____

🎧 Now listen and check your answers. Change the false statements to true ones.

B. GROUPS

- Take turns saying the facts. Then close your books.
- How many facts can you remember? Say all the facts you remember.

A. PAIRS Answer the questions. Then ask your partner. Add information.

Example: A: *What kind of jewelry do you wear?*
              B: *I wear a watch and a ring. That's all. What about you?*
              A: *I love to wear jewelry. I wear earrings, necklaces, rings, and watches.*

	YOU	YOUR PARTNER
• What kind of jewelry do you wear?		
• What's your favorite piece of jewelry?		
• Where do you buy jewelry?		
• Did you ever make jewelry?		

Tell the class one thing about your partner.
Example: *Jay doesn't wear jewelry.*

B. WHOLE CLASS Survey four students.

Ask: What kind of jewelry looks good on men?
       What doesn't look good? a chain? a bracelet?
       an earring? a nose ring? an eyebrow ring?

Report the results to the class.
Example: *Erika thinks chains and bracelets look
              good on men. She doesn't like eyebrow
              rings or earrings.*

Give Your Opinion

A. Listen to the opinion. Then listen to the responses.

A man wants to buy his girlfriend a diamond ring for their engagement, but she doesn't want a ring. She wants a motorcycle instead. I say get her a motorcycle.

I disagree. A ring lasts forever. A motorcycle doesn't. When she gets the ring, she will love it.

I agree. Not everyone likes diamond rings. A motorcycle is much more fun.

B. PAIRS Do you agree with the man or the woman? Add your opinion.
Example: A: *I agree with the woman. I think I'd prefer a motorcycle, too.*
              B: *I disagree . . .*

Responses
I agree.
I disagree.

Listening Comprehension 1

Warm up: How do people decide the value of a diamond?

 Listen to a talk about diamonds. Then listen again, and change these false statements to true ones.

1. The four Cs are carat, clarity, color, and class.
2. Carat means size.
3. The worst diamonds are the clearest.
4. The most expensive diamonds have the most color.
5. Some diamond salespeople say, "Spend one month's salary on an engagement ring."

Conversation Practice   Information Gap

PAIRS Student A, turn to page 106. Student B, turn to page 108.

Listening Comprehension 2

Warm up: What do you know about the Hope Diamond?

Weight: 45.52 carats
Color: dark blue
Clarity: perfect
Cut: oval Brilliant

 Listen to a radio program about the Hope Diamond. Then answer the questions.

1. What are two reasons the Hope Diamond is famous?
2. What do people say about the Hope Diamond?
3. Where does it come from?
4. Where is it today?
5. Can people see it?

Check This Out

A. GROUPS What do you know about the Tower of London. Try to complete the sentences. (Check your answers on page 107.)

1. In the past, the Tower of London was a _____.

   a. hotel   b. prison

2. People tried to steal the Crown Jewels _____.

   a. once   b. twice

3. Beefeaters _____ the Tower of London.

   a. guard   b. repair

Unit 5 Emergencies and Disasters

Do you like disaster movies? Do you know these movies?

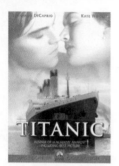

Titanic, 1996   *Volcano, 1997*   *The Perfect Storm, 2000*

Facts

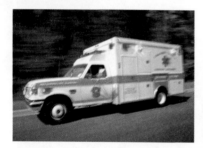

A. GROUPS Try to complete the sentences. Use the phrases in the box.

earthquake	typhoons	emergency	hurricanes	E.R. (emergency room)	ambulance

<u>Were you right?</u>

1. Something dangerous happens. You need to act now.   _____

   You say, "This is an _____."
2. You need to get to a hospital. You call an _____.   _____
3. People in an accident are taken to the _____ in a hospital.   _____
4. The earth shakes during an _____.   _____
5. Strong storms in the Atlantic Ocean or Caribbean Sea are called _____.   _____
6. Strong storms in the Pacific Ocean or Indian Ocean are called _____.   _____

🎧 **Now listen and check your answers.**

B. GROUPS

- Take turns saying the facts. Then close your books.
- How many facts can you remember? Say all the facts you remember.

Talk about Your Experience

A. PAIRS Answer the questions. Then ask your partner. Add information.

Example: *A: How do you act after an emergency?*
             B: I talk a lot about it. Then I feel better.

	YOU	YOUR PARTNER
• Were you ever in an earthquake? a fire? a bad storm? When? Where? What happened?		
• After an emergency, people act in different ways. They cry, laugh, eat, exercise, sleep, talk a lot about it, or don't talk about it. How do you act?		

Tell the class one thing about your partner's experience.

Example: *There was a terrible storm. A tree fell on Ranya's car. She was OK, but the car*
             was badly damaged.

B. WHOLE CLASS Survey the class.

A blackout means there is no electricity and the lights go out. Imagine a blackout in your class right now. Find someone who has the following things. Ask: Do you have . . . ?

a. matches
b. a flashlight
c. a candle
d. a laptop
e. a radio
f. batteries
g. food
f. a cell phone

Give Your Opinion

A. 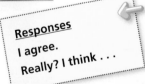 Listen to the opinion. Then listen to the responses.

All disaster movies are alike.

I agree. The stories are very similar.

Really? I think the stories are different. They're alike in only two ways—there's a disaster and some people live and some die.

B. PAIRS Do you agree with the man or the woman? Add your opinion.

Example: *A: I think the man is right. All disaster movies are alike.*
             I think they are boring.
             B: Really? I think . . .

> **Responses**
> I agree.
> Really? I think . . .

Warm up: Are there a lot of blackouts in your area? What things are good to have in a blackout?

A. 🎧 **Marco asks his friend Karen about a blackout. Listen to their telephone conversation. Then listen again, and answer the questions.**

1. Where was the blackout?

   a. in Mexico   b. in Ohio

2. Where was the woman?

   a. at work   b. at home

3. What was she doing?

   a. sending a fax   b. fixing her fax machine

4. What did her husband say?

   a. "Karen, what did you do?"   b. "Karen, are you OK?"

5. What did they eat?

   a. ice cream   b. candy

6. How did they eat?

   a. without light   b. without spoons

B. PAIRS Now take turns telling the story in your own words.

Begin like this: "There was a blackout in _____. Karen was _____."

Conversation Practice

A. PAIRS Look at the pictures. What would you do? Circle the correct picture. Explain your answer. (Check your answers on page 107.)

1. There is a fire in a building. You are on a high floor.

   a   b

3. There is an earthquake.

   a   b

2. There is a fire and a lot of smoke.

   a   b

4. There is an earthquake.

   a   b

B. PAIRS Now make a list.

What to do in an Emergency:

1. *In case of fire, take the stairs. Don't take the elevator.* _____

2. _____

3. _____

4. _____

Warm up: What do you know about forest fires?

 Listen to a talk about forest fires in Canada. Then complete the chart.

Canadian Forest Fires	
Month grass fires start	
Month forest fires end	
Amount of land burned each year	_____ square kilometers
Number of fires each year	
People who fight fires	_____ and _____
Percent of fires that people cause	_____ %

Check This Out

GROUPS Do you understand these signs? Match the signs with the meanings.

DANGER KEEP OUT	POISON	BEWARE OF DOG	EMERGENCY EXIT
_d_	_____	_____	_____

a. Do not drink.

b. A dog may bite you.

c. This is a way to leave.

d. Do not enter.

When you were a child, who read to you?

My mother ☐

My father ☐

A sister or brother ☐

A teacher ☐

A babysitter ☐

Someone else ☐

Facts

A. GROUPS Guess which statements are true (T) and which statements are false (F).

<u>Your answer</u>   <u>Were you right?</u>

_____ 1. Fables are stories about machines that talk.   _____

_____ 2. Aesop's Fables are over 2,300 years old. Aesop was from Italy.   _____

_____ 3. There are many presidents, queens, princes, and princesses in fairy tales.   _____

_____ 4. Fairy tales often begin, "Once upon a time . . ."   _____

_____ 5. Fairy tales often end, "They lived quietly ever after."   _____

_____ 6. Hans Christian Andersen wrote *The Little Mermaid* and *The Ugly Duckling*.   _____

🎧 Now listen and check your answers. Change the false statements to true ones.

B. GROUPS

- Take turns saying the facts. Then close your books.
- How many facts can you remember? Say all the facts you remember.

Talk about Your Experience

A. PAIRS Answer the questions. Then ask your partner. Add information.

Example: A: *What's your favorite fairy tale or fable?*
B: *I love* Little Red Riding Hood. *It's about a little girl who meets a wolf on the way to her grandmother's house.*

	YOU	YOUR PARTNER
• What's your favorite fairy tale or fable? What is it about?		
• Did a story ever scare you? What was it about?		
• Do you like to read to children? Why or why not?		
• Do you like to write your own stories?		

Tell the class about your partner.

Example: *My partner's favorite fairy tale is* The Frog Princess. *It's a Russian story about a prince who marries a frog. The frog turns into a beautiful princess.*

B. GROUPS Find three classmates who know the same fable, fairy tale, or children's story. Write as much as you can about it.

Example: Heidi *is a story about a young girl. She lives in Switzerland. She lives in the mountains. She lives with her . . .*

Read your work to the class.

Give Your Opinion

A. 🎧 Listen to the opinion. Then listen to the responses.

> **Most fairy tales are too scary for young children.**

> I think that's true. I remember crying and worrying after I heard the story of *Hansel and Gretel.*

> I don't agree. I think children love fairy tales with scary parts.

B. PAIRS Do you agree with the man or the woman? Add your opinion.

Example: A: *I agree with the woman. As a child, some fairy tales gave me bad dreams.*
B: *I don't agree . . .*

Responses
I think that's true.
I don't agree.

A. 🎧 *The Ugly Duckling* **is a story by Hans Christian Andersen. Listen to the story. Mark the statements true (T) or false (F). Then change the false statements to true ones.**

_____ 1. A mother hen sat on her eggs.

_____ 2. One of her babies was big and ugly.

_____ 3. The other ducks said: "You're big and beautiful."

_____ 4. He felt bad all winter long.

_____ 5. During the winter he changed.

_____ 6. He became a beautiful sea gull.

_____ 7. Some say the story is a lot like Andersen's life.

_____ 8. Andersen was born poor but later became rich.

B. GROUPS Why do people like this story? What is the message? Do you like it? Why or why not?

Conversation Practice

A. PAIRS **A miser is a person who does not like to spend money. Read this story about a miser. Make up an ending for the story.**

The Miser

Once upon a time, a miser sold all he had and bought a lump of gold. He buried the gold in a hole in the ground. Every day after that, he went to look at his gold. One of the miser's workmen watched the miser and saw the gold. The next night the workman stole the gold. When the miser found the hole empty, he began to shout and scream. A neighbor heard the story and said to the miser:

B. 🎧 **Now listen to the story with the ending.**

A. PAIRS This story is from Aesop's Fables. Look at the pictures. What do you think the story is about? Tell the story in your own words.

B. Listen to the story. What is the message? What do you think of it?

Check This Out

GROUPS Maurice Sendak draws monsters for children's books. Children love his drawings, but some people say they are too scary for children.

What do you think about this drawing?

Unit 7   Gestures

What are they saying?
(Check your answers on page 107.)

a.   b.

How do you show you don't believe someone?
How do you show you are angry?

Facts

A. GROUPS Try to complete the sentences.

Were you right?

1. Gestures are one kind of _____.

   a. body language   b. joke   c. secret message

   _____

2. In Asia, a smile sometimes means you are _____.

   a. hungry   b. thirsty   c. embarrassed

   _____

3. In most countries, moving your head up and down means "yes."
   But in Bulgaria it means _____.

   a. "no"   b. "I love you"   c. "hi"

   _____

   _____

4. At plays, lectures, and concerts in Europe, some people _____ when they don't
   like something.

   a. cough   b. whistle   c. laugh

   _____

5. Business people in the United States shake hands _____ and look you in the eye.

   a. gently   b. firmly   c. carefully

   _____

🎧 **Now listen and check your answers.**

B. GROUPS

- Take turns saying the facts. Then close your books.
- How many facts can you remember? Say all the facts you remember.

A. PAIRS Answer the questions. Then ask your partner. Add information.

Example: A: *What can you "say" without words?*
B: *I'm happy, I'm hungry, and I'm thirsty.*

	YOU	YOUR PARTNER
• Which of these can you "say" without words? • I'm happy. • I'm angry. • I'm tired. • I'm hungry. • I'm thirsty. • I'm sorry. • I don't know. • I don't care. • Now "say" one of the above without words. • Can your partner understand your body language?		

Make a gesture. Your class gives the meaning in words.

B. WHOLE CLASS Make a list of gestures. Decide who uses the gesture more often, men or women.

Gestures Used by Men and Women	Gestures Used More Often by Men	Gestures Used More Often by Women

Example: *Women smile more often than men.*

Give Your Opinion

A. 🎧 Listen to the opinion. Then listen to the responses.

> **Women understand body language better than men.**

> I agree.
> I think women look at people more closely.

> I disagree. I think men understand men's body language, and women understand women's body language.

B. PAIRS Do you agree with the man or the woman? Add your opinion.

Example: A: *I think the man is right. Women usually pay more attention to body language than men.*
B: *I disagree . . .*

Responses
I agree.
I disagree.

Warm up: Are there gestures that everyone understands?

Roger G. Axtell is the author of many popular books about body language. He says, "There is one gesture that people everywhere use." Listen. Then decide what gesture the speaker is talking about.

The gesture is _____.

(Check your answer on page 107).

Conversation Practice

A. PAIRS Take turns. Choose one of the statements below, and use gestures to express it. Your partner says what it is.

Example: A: *What am I saying?*
              B: *Is it, "I don't know?"*
              A: *Yes, it is. You're right.*

1. I don't know.   4. Stop.
2. Hi.   5. Come here.
3. Money.   6. Me?

B. PAIRS Label these body parts. Use the words in the box. (Check your answers on page 107.)

head	eye	eyebrow	nose	mouth	shoulder
hand	arm	finger	leg	foot	

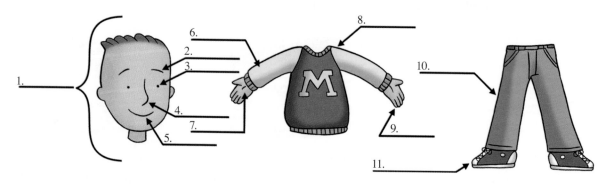

What parts of the body did you use to make the gestures in Part A?

Warm up: When do you shake hands? Is your handshake strong? When do you touch a person's arm or back? When is it OK to interrupt a person during a conversation?

GROUPS Listen to information about customs in Brazil. Then listen again and complete the chart.

Country	Greeting	Other Customs
Brazil	People _____ _____ when they meet. It lasts a _____ time. They _____ hands when they say _____ and _____. They use good _____ contact. They shake the hand of _____ in a room.	It's OK to _____ other people's _____, _____, and backs. It's OK to interrupt during a conversation. It shows you are _____.

Check This Out

GROUPS Do you understand these American gestures? What do they mean? Write the answer on the line. (Check your answers on page 107.)

1. _____

2. _____

3. _____

4. _____

a. Stop.
b. I can't hear you.
c. Be quiet (usually for children).
d. I've had enough to eat.

Do you use these gestures? Do your friends use them?

Which hairstyles do you prefer?

a.   b.
Halle Berry

a.   b.
Mark McGrath

a.   b.
Serena Williams

Facts

A. GROUPS Guess which statements are true (T) and which statements are false (F).

Your answer   **Were you right?**

_____ 1. The average head has 100,000 hairs.

_____ 2. The average person loses about 100 hairs a day.   _____

_____ 3. Someone without hair is bold.   _____

_____ 4. Hair grows faster in cold weather.   _____

_____ 5. British nurses wear wigs.   _____

🎧 **Now listen and check your answers. Change the false statements to true ones.**

B. GROUPS

• Take turns saying the facts. Then close your books.
• How many facts can you remember? Say all the facts you remember.

A. PAIRS Answer the questions. Then ask your partner. Add information.

Example: A: *How often do you get a haircut?*
B: *Once a month.*

	YOU	YOUR PARTNER
• How often do you get a haircut?		
• Did you ever have an unusual hairstyle? What was it? Did your friends like it? Why or why not?		
• What was your worst hairstyle?		

Tell the class about your partner.
Example: *Takako dyed her hair blonde. She liked it, but her friends didn't.*

B. WHOLE CLASS Survey two men and two women.
Ask: Did you ever have:
    a. a shaved head?
    b. very short hair?
    c. very long hair?
    d. very curly hair?
    e. red, yellow, green, or blue hair?

Report the results to the class.
Example: *Hiro had a shaved head two years ago. Juanita had bright red hair for one week in high school. Sun Mi has very short hair now. Pierre always has very long hair.*

Give Your Opinion

A. 🎧 **Listen to the opinion. Then listen to the responses.**

You should change your hairstyle every six months.

I don't think so.
I think some people look good
in one style.

I think so, too.
It's boring to always wear the
same hairstyle.

B. PAIRS Do you agree with the man or the woman? Add your opinion.
Example: A: *I think the woman is right. Everyone can look good in different styles.*
B: *I don't think so . . .*

Responses
I think so, too.
I don't think so.

🎧 A woman calls for an appointment at Renée's Hair Salon. Listen to the conversation. Then complete the information.

RENÉE'S
Hair Salon

Cut and Style — $60.00
Color — $60.00 and up

Name of customer: _____

Time and day of appointment: _____

Customer wants: _____

Conversation Practice

PAIRS Look at the pictures.
Which styles do you like? Why?

Listening Comprehension 2

Warm up: Do judges wear wigs in all countries?

🎧 **Listen to a talk about wigs in Great Britain. Then complete the sentences.**

1. Judges in Great Britain started to wear wigs in the _____.

2. The wigs are made of _____.

3. They are not _____.

4. Judges don't have to _____ for their wigs.

5. Some wigs are expensive because they belonged to _____ judges.

Check This Out

GROUPS **What do you think of these hairstyles? When would someone wear these hairstyles?**

This is the largest ice hotel in the world.
It is in Sweden.
It's open from October to April.

Would you like to stay at an ice hotel?
Why or why not?

Facts

A. GROUPS Try to complete the sentences.

Were you right?

1. Ice is _____ water.

   a. the same weight as   b. heavier than   c. lighter than   _____

2. The ice age started _____ million years ago and ended 11,000 years ago.   _____

   a. 1   b. 2   c. 3

3. An iceberg is a large piece of ice moving in the ocean. Almost _____ of an iceberg is below water.   _____

   a. 50%   b. 70%   c. 90%

4. The native people of Northern Canada used to live in _____.   _____

   a. igloos   b. huts   c. tents

5. When you meet people and say something that makes them feel comfortable, you are "_____ the ice."   _____

   a. breaking   b. covering   c. hitting

6. When you want a drink with ice cubes, you ask for a drink "on the _____."   _____

   a. cubes   b. rocks   c. cold

   Now listen and check your answers.

B. GROUPS

• Take turns saying the facts. Then close your books.
• How many facts can you remember? Say all the facts you remember.

Talk about Your Experience

A. PAIRS Answer the questions. Then ask your partner. Add information.

Example: A: *Do you like cold weather?*
B: *No, I don't. I like warm weather.*

	YOU	YOUR PARTNER

• Do you like cold weather?
  Do you like snow?
 	
• Did you watch these sports during the
  Winter Olympics?
 	
  • ice skating
  • ice hockey
  • skiing
  • snowboarding
  • sledding
 	
• Do you like to do any of these sports?
  If so, which ones?
  Do you like any other winter sports?		

Tell the class one thing about your partner.

Example: *Elena watched ice skating and skiing during the last Winter Olympics.*

B. WHOLE CLASS Survey five students.

Ask: What do you do on a cold winter day?

_____ take a long walk   _____ stay indoors and watch TV

_____ do a winter sport   _____ other

Report the results to the class. What do most of your classmates do?

Give Your Opinion

A. 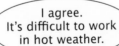 **Listen to the opinion. Then listen to the responses.**

It's easier to work or study when the weather is cold.

I agree. It's difficult to work in hot weather.

Really? I think people work when they want to. The weather isn't important.

B. PAIRS Do you agree with the man or the woman? Add your opinion.

Example: A: *I agree with the man. When it's hot, most people want*
to relax.
B: *I agree . . .*

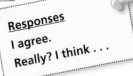

Responses
I agree.
Really? I think . . .

Warm up: The man is making an ice sculpture. What do you know about ice sculptures?

🎧 **Listen to a talk about an artist who does ice sculptures. Then answer the questions.**

1. When did Duncan begin ice sculpting? _____.

2. What did he do before he was a sculptor? _____.

3. How long do his sculptures last? They usually last _____.

4. When do the sculptures look best? They look best when _____.

5. Why doesn't Duncan feel bad when they melt? He thinks of the sculptures _____.

Conversation Practice

A. PAIRS How do you start a conversation with a stranger? Complete the first four sentences. Then write your own sentence.

1. The weather is very _____, isn't it?

2. Do you _____ here? (live/work/study)

3. Are there any good _____ near here?

4. Are you _____ this class? (in/taking)

5. _____.

B. WHOLE CLASS Move around the room. Pretend you are at a party and you don't know anyone. Start conversations. Use the sentences from Exercise A.

C. WHOLE CLASS Discuss which sentences are good icebreakers.

Warm up: Read these questions about some of Canada's native people, the Inuit. Can you answer any of them?

1. What does the word "Inuit" mean?

    a. real people   b. rain people

2. When did the Inuit get their own land from the Canadian government?

    a. 1989   b. 1999

3. How many people live in Nunavut?

    a. 62,000   b. 26,000

4. Do most Inuit live in igloos?

    a. no   b. yes

5. How do they travel?

    a. dog sleds and trains   b. snowmobiles and planes

6. How do the Inuit keep old ideas?

    a. old people tell stories   b. young people read books

7. What are two parts of their lives that continue to be important?

    a. TV and movies   b. the family and nature

 Listen to a talk about the lives of the people in Nunavut. Then circle the correct answers.

Check This Out

GROUPS These men are building an igloo for fun. Would you like to build an igloo? Why or why not? Would you like to sleep in one?

When you throw something away, it can stay in the ground for a long time. A glass bottle stays in the ground a million years. Do you think about this when you throw things away?

A banana peel	stays in the ground for **1 to 2 weeks.**
Wool socks	stays in the ground for **1 to 5 years.**
A plastic bag	stays in the ground for **10 to 20 years.**
An aluminum can	stays in the ground for **80 to 100 years.**
A glass bottle	stays in the ground for **1,000,000 years.**

Source: Adapted from *Science World,* vol. 57, No. 13—Scholastic (Graph)

Facts

A. GROUPS Guess which statements are true (T) and which statements are false (F).

<u>Your answer</u>   <u>Were you right?</u>

_____ 1. Soda, candy, and potato chips are examples of junk food.   _____

_____ 2. Companies send mail we don't want. We call this mail junk mail.   _____
             Americans throw away 44% of this mail without opening it.

_____ 3. E-mail ads are called ham.   _____

_____ 4. A market with old or used things is a flea market.   _____

_____ 5. People put things in front of their houses and sell them at a garage sale. _____

_____ 6. When you use something again, you bicycle it.   _____

🎧 **Now listen and check your answers. Change the false statements to true ones.**

B. GROUPS

- Take turns saying the facts. Then close your books.
- How many facts can you remember? Say all the facts you remember.

Talk about Your Experience

A. PAIRS Answer the questions. Then ask your partner. Add information.

Example: A: *Is it easy for you to throw away things?*

B: *Yes and no. I can throw away things like e-mail messages, but I can't throw away letters or cards from friends.*

	YOU	YOUR PARTNER

• Is it easy for you to throw away things?
 	
• Do you throw away
  • letters or cards from friends?
  • clothes?
  • pictures?
  • e–mail messages?
  • videos or DVDs?
 	
• Do you ever buy secondhand (used) things?
  If you do, what used things do you buy?		

Tell the class one thing about your partner.

Example: *Kimiko never throws away pictures. She has ten albums of photographs.*

B. WHOLE CLASS Survey five students.

Ask:

Do you keep too many things?   Do you have enough space for all your things?

Do you throw away too many things?   Do you know someone who cannot throw things away?

Report the results to the class.

Example: *Juan keeps too many things. He doesn't have enough space for all his things.*

Give Your Opinion

A. Listen to the opinion. Then listen to the responses.

> **It's fun to shop at flea markets.**

> Do you really think so? I think there's a lot of junk at flea markets. And prices are often high.

> I agree. I always find something old and interesting at flea markets.

B. PAIRS Do you agree with the man or the woman? Add your opinion.

Example: A: *I agree with the woman. I love to shop at flea markets. The things there are often unusual.*

B: *Do you really think so? I think . . .*

Responses

I agree.

Do you really think so?

I think . . .

Warm up: This is a photo of "space junk." What do you know about space junk?

🎧 **Listen to a talk about space junk. Then complete the sentences.**

1. The light in Tasmania was either a shooting _____ or _____ junk.
2. Scientists know about over _____ pieces of junk in space.
3. _____ has been hurt by space junk yet.
4. Scientists are keeping _____ of space junk.
5. Scientists know what to do about space junk, but they don't do it now because it _____ too much.

Conversation Practice

A. PAIRS Environmentalists are people who want to protect nature, the land, sea, and air. Read these ideas from environmentalists. Why do they say these things? Discuss with a partner.

1. Using electricity is better than using batteries.
2. A ten-minute bath is better than a ten-minute shower.
3. Cloth towels are better than paper towels.
4. A microwave oven is better than a regular oven.
5. A bicycle is better than a car.

B. WHOLE CLASS Discuss your answers with the class.
Do you think the environmentalists are right?
What do you do?

Warm up: What do you do when you get a gift that you don't like?

🎧 **Listen to this story. Then listen again, and complete the sentences.**

A few months after Janet was married, her grandmother gave her a _____. Janet didn't like the _____. One day she decided to _____ it away. A _____ later she met a _____. Janet and the woman became _____. The woman _____ Janet for _____. When Janet came to her home, she saw her grandmother's _____. Janet smiled, but she didn't say anything to her new friend. Several _____ later she went to a store. She saw the same lamp. It was very _____. She discovered her grandmother's _____ was an antique.

Were you ever sorry that you threw away something?

Check This Out

GROUPS Do you have a lot of papers? When you have papers, do you keep them in piles or files? Why?

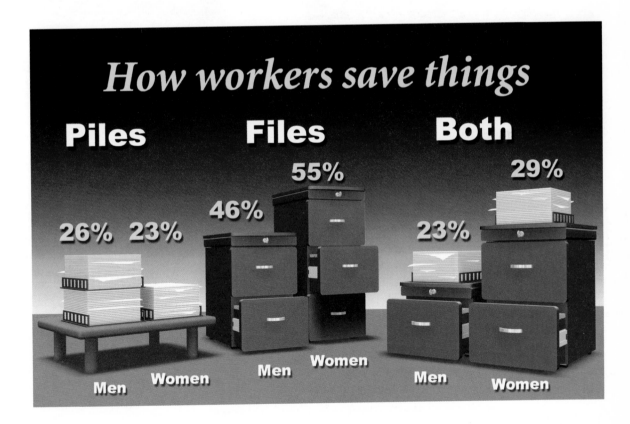

Unit 11 — Kandinsky, Klee, and Modern Art

Look at this painting.
Do you like it?
Why or why not?

Paul Klee, *Seafarer*

Facts

Wassily Kandinsky, *The Cavalier*

Paul Klee, *Comedy*

A. GROUPS Try to complete the sentences.

Were you right?

1. Kandinsky was one of the first _____ artists. _____

   a. abstract   b. realistic   c. Russian

2. Klee's paintings are not _____. _____

   a. small and delicate   b. big and bold   c. childlike

3. Paul Klee was born in _____ in 1879. _____

   a. France   b. Sweden   c. Switzerland

4. Wassily Kandinsky was born in Moscow in _____. _____

   a. 1866   b. 1896   c. 1926

5. Before he became an artist, Kandinsky studied _____ at the University of Moscow. _____

   a. law   b. medicine   c. engineering

6. Klee and Kandinsky were _____. _____

   a. friends   b. cousins   c. business partners

🎧 **Now listen and check your answers.**

B. GROUPS

- Take turns saying the facts. Then close your books.
- How many facts can you remember? Say all the facts you remember.

A. PAIRS Answer the questions. Then ask your partner. Add information.

Example: A: *Do you like modern art?*

B: *It depends. I like some modern art, but not all.*

	YOU	YOUR PARTNER
• Do you like modern art?		
• Do you enjoy going to art museums?		
• Name three artists you like. What do you like about their work?		
• Do you like to • draw? • paint? • sculpt? • take photographs?		
• As a child, were you good at art?		

Tell the class one thing about your partner.

Example: *Rene likes to sculpt. He has sculptures all over his apartment.*

B. WHOLE CLASS Discuss the following questions.

1. Can people learn to be artists?
2. Is it hard to be an artist? Why or why not?
3. Why do people become artists?

Give Your Opinion

A. 🎧 Listen to the opinion. Then listen to the responses.

Art does not have to be beautiful.

I agree.
Art has to make you feel something. It can make you feel things without being beautiful.

I disagree.
I think art has to be beautiful.

B. PAIRS Do you agree with the man or the woman? Add your opinion.

Example: A: *I think the woman is right. For me art has to be beautiful.*

B: *I disagree . . .*

Responses
I agree.
I disagree.

Listening Comprehension 1

Warm up: Kandinsky (1866–1944) and Klee (1879–1940) lived around the same time. Are they alike in any other ways?

Listen to a talk about the artists. Check (✓) the ways that they were alike.

_____ 1. Both men came from athletic families.

_____ 2. Both men taught at the Bauhaus school in Germany.

_____ 3. Both men had many children.

_____ 4. Music was important for both men.

_____ 5. Both men were poor.

_____ 6. Both men wrote about art.

_____ 7. Both men had many talents.

Conversation Practice

PAIRS Read the information below.

In 1998 a Van Gogh painting sold for $71.5 million.
In 1990 a Renior painting sold for $78.1 million.
In 1990 a Van Gogh painting sold for $82.5 million.

What do you think?

• Is any painting worth so much money?

• Why or why not?

• Why do people buy these paintings?

Listening Comprehension 2

Warm up: Sometimes a piece of art is hard to understand. What questions help you understand art?

Listen to a talk about understanding art. Then complete the questions.

1. How is this art like _____ art?

2. What do you know about the _____?

3. When and where was this art _____?

4. Does it tell a _____?

   Does it tell about a _____, a _____, or an _____?

5. Does this art make you _____ or _____ anything?

6. What is this art _____ of?

Look at this painting by Kandinsky. Look back at the questions in Listening Comprehension 2. Do the questions help you understand the painting? Why or why not? Do you like the painting?

Wassily Kandinsky, *Contrasting Sounds*, 1924

Unit 12 Laughter

What makes you laugh?

a funny TV show   a comedian   a comic book

Facts

A. GROUPS Try to complete the sentences.

Were you right?

1. The average person laughs _____ times a day.

   a. five   b. ten   c. thirteen   _____

2. Both chimpanzees and baby _____ laugh.

   a. birds   b. rats   c. elephants   _____

3. A baby begins to laugh at _____ months.

   a. two   b. four   c. six   _____

4. "Laughter is the best _____" is a famous saying.

   a. medicine   b. message   c. mirror   _____

5. When you are not serious about something, you say, "I'm just _____."

   a. playing   b. kidding   c. imagining   _____

6. When you "get" a joke, you _____ it.

   a. like   b. understand   c. buy   _____

   Now listen and check your answers.

B. GROUPS

- Take turns saying the facts. Then close your books.
- How many facts can you remember? Say all the facts you remember.

A. PAIRS Answer the questions. Then ask your partner. Add information.

Example: A: *What's a funny movie?*

B: *Shrek. I saw it four times. I laughed each time I saw it.*

	YOU	YOUR PARTNER
• What's a funny movie? What's a funny TV show? Who's your favorite comedian? • Do you have a funny friend? Why is this person funny? • Do you have a friend who laughs at the same things you do? What kinds of things do you laugh at? • Who's the funniest person in your family?		

Tell the class one thing about your partner.

Example: *Xavier's best friend is funny. His friend is a comedian.*

B. WHOLE CLASS

Some movies or books make you laugh. Some movies or books make you cry. What kind of movies do you prefer? Why?

Example: A: *I like funny movies. When I go to the movies, I want to feel good.*

B: *I like both funny and sad movies. A movie like* Life Is Beautiful *is both funny and sad.*

Give Your Opinion

A. 🎧 **Listen to the opinion. Then listen to the responses.**

Laughter is the best medicine.

I think so, too. When I'm sick, I always watch funny movies.

I don't think so. I think that laughter doesn't always make you feel better.

B. PAIRS Do you agree with the man or the woman? Add your opinion.

Example: A: *I think the woman is right. Laughter helps me forget that I'm sick.*

B: *I don't think so . . .*

Responses
I think so, too.
I don't think so.

Listening Comprehension 1

Warm up: You will hear these words in the listening. Do you know what they mean? If not, look them up in a dictionary.

surprise	relief	stress	tension

🎧 **Listen to a talk about what makes people laugh. Then complete the sentences.**

1. People laugh when there is a _____. They expect _____ thing, but something else _____.

2. People laugh at other people's _____.

3. People laugh when they feel _____ from stress.

Conversation Practice

A. Read the beginning of this story.

Once there was a mother cat and three baby kittens. The mother cat said to her kittens, "It's a beautiful day. Go take a walk." The kittens walked for a while when they saw a dog. The dog looked at the baby kittens and barked, "Woof, woof." The kittens ran back home. Their mother said, "Why are you here?" The kittens replied, "Meow, meow. There was a big dog. He barked at us and scared us." The mother cat said, "Come with me." So the mother cat and the kittens started to walk. Again the dog appeared and barked at the four cats.

B. PAIRS This is the end of the story. The sentences are not in the correct order. Put them in the correct order. Write 1–4. Then read the story aloud.

_____ The dog walked away.

_____ Now the mother cat smiled at her kittens and said, "Watch me."

_____ The cat turned to her kittens and said, "Now you see the importance of a second language!"

_____ Then she looked the dog in his eyes and said, "Woof, woof."

C. 🎧 **WHOLE CLASS** Now listen to the story. Do you like the story? Is it funny?

Warm up: Why is it good to laugh? How can you put more laughter in your life?

🎧 **Listen to a talk about laughter. Check (✓) the ideas you hear.**

_____ 1. Almost everyone says it's good to smile.

_____ 2. Scientists say laughter is good for your health.

_____ 3. Laughter makes you feel smart.

_____ 4. Laughter and exercise lower blood pressure.

_____ 5. Laughter and exercise make your legs move faster.

_____ 6. To put more laughter in your life, decide what makes you laugh.

_____ 7. To put more laughter in your life, meet with people who make you sing.

Check This Out

GROUPS People laugh in different ways. How do you laugh?

Did anyone teach you how to laugh?

Can you match the mask and the country? (Check your answers on page 107.)

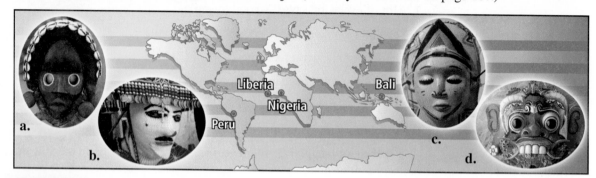

Facts

A. GROUPS Try to complete the sentences.   Were you right?

1. Both Brazil and _____ have celebrations with masks and costumes.   _____
   a. Vienna   b. Venice   c. Victoria

2. Children in Canada and the United States wear costumes and masks on _____.   _____
   a. Thanksgiving   b. Halloween   c. Mother's Day

3. *Noh* theater started in Japan in the 14th century. In *Noh* plays, the main actors   _____
   wear masks. All the actors are _____.
   a. men   b. women   c. children

4. On the Chinese New Year people wear masks and costumes and do a _____ dance.   _____
   a. tiger   b. lion   c. zebra

5. A _____ does not wear a mask.   _____
   a. dentist   b. doctor   c. lawyer

   🎧 **Now listen and check your answers.**

B. GROUPS
- Take turns saying the facts. Then close your books.
- How many facts can you remember? Say all the facts you remember.

Talk about Your Experience

A. PAIRS Answer the questions. Then ask your partner. Add information.

Example: A: *Do you have any masks?*
B. *Yes. I have one. I bought it in New Orleans.*
A. *What does it look like?*
B: *It's colorful and has feathers.*

	YOU	YOUR PARTNER
• Do you have any masks? Did you make or buy them? What do they look like?		
• Do you like costume parties? Why or why not? Did you ever make a costume? What was it?		
• Is makeup like a mask? If so, how?		

Tell the class about yourself and your partner.
Example: *We both like costume parties. We enjoy making and wearing unusual costumes.*

B. WHOLE CLASS
Do people in your country wear masks? What kinds? When do they wear them?

Give Your Opinion

A. 🎧 Listen to the opinion. Then listen to the responses.

> Costume parties are for children.

> I disagree. I think costume parties are for everyone.

> I agree. Costume parties are silly. I never wear a mask or a costume anymore.

B. PAIRS Do you agree with the man or the woman? Add your opinion.
Example: A: *I agree with the man. I love to wear a costume. I think costume parties are a lot of fun.*
B: *I disagree . . .*

> **Responses**
> I agree.
> I disagree.

Warm up: What city is this?

C. 🎧 **Listen to a talk about this city. Then complete the sentences.**

1. The Venice Carnival takes place in the month of _____.
2. People wear _____ at the Carnival.
3. The modern Venice Carnival began in the _____.
4. In the past in Venice people used to wear _____ all the time.
5. Venetians used to be _____ and powerful.
6. The Venetian Republic ended by the end of the _____ century.

Conversation Practice

GROUPS Your class is having a costume party. Plan a mask and costume for everyone in your group. Tell the other groups about your costumes and masks. Tell as much as you can about them. The class decides on the best and most unusual costumes.

Warm up: Masks are important in many places in Africa. Look at this African mask. What does it look like to you?

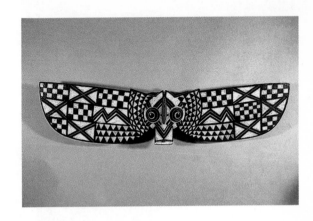

🎧 **Listen to a talk about the mask. Check (✓) all the things you hear.**

_____ 1. This is an animal mask.

_____ 2. This mask is from Bermuda.

_____ 3. This mask is from Burkino Faso.

_____ 4. This mask is worn by the Nuna people.

_____ 5. The masks of the Nuna people have large noses and three eyes.

_____ 6. Dancers wear these masks on wedding days.

_____ 7. Dancers wear these masks when someone dies.

_____ 8. People sing and play drums while the dancers dance.

Check This Out

GROUPS The Yup'ik are native Alaskans. These are three of their masks. During the long dark winter in Alaska, men danced and told stories wearing these and other masks.

What words describe these masks?

    a. funny
    b. sad
    c. angry
    d. strange

What do you think the masks are made of?

What do the masks look like?

Do you like them?

Unit 14 — Names, Nicknames, and Titles

Can you match the nicknames with the photos? (Check your answers on page 107.)

Shaq
Guga
Magic
Godzilla

Hideki Matsui

Gustavo Kuerten

Shaquille O'Neal

Earvin Johnson

Do you know the nicknames of other athletes?

Facts

A. GROUPS Guess which statements are true (T) and which statements are false (F).

Your answer		Were you right?
_____	1. We use the title Ms. before a married man or woman's name.	_____
_____	2. In North America, a person's family name is his or her first name.	_____
_____	3. The initials of Johann Sebastian Bach are GSB.	_____
_____	4. A professor teaches at an elementary or middle school.	_____
_____	5. Some writers give themselves pen names.	_____
_____	6. In Canada and the United States, it's incorrect to call a teacher "Teacher."	_____

🎧 **Now listen and check your answers. Change the false statements to true ones.**

B. GROUPS

- Take turns saying the facts. Then close your books.
- How many facts can you remember? Say all the facts you remember.

Talk about Your Experience

A. PAIRS Answer the questions. Then ask your partner. Add information.

> *Example:*   A: *Does your name have a special meaning?*
> B: *Yes. My name is Fortunato. It means "fortunate" or "blessed."*

	YOU	YOUR PARTNER
• Do you like your name? Does it have a special meaning? How did your parents choose your name? Is your name common or unusual?		
• Do you have a nickname or did you ever have one? How did you get your nickname?		
• Is your name hard for people to pronounce?		

Tell the class about your partner.

Example: *My partner's name is Fortunato. He was named after his grandfather.*

B. WHOLE CLASS Survey five students.

Ask: How do you feel when . . .

	I feel upset.	I feel angry.	It's OK.
someone forgets your name?			
someone mispronounces your name?			
someone calls you by the wrong name?			

Report the results to the class.

Give Your Opinion

A. 🎧 **Listen to the opinion. Then listen to the responses.**

> **It's important to remember names.**

> I think so, too. I didn't remember Nora's name and she was angry.

> I don't think so. My friend Bob can't remember names. He remembers faces.

B. PAIRS Do you agree with the man or the woman? Add your opinion.

Example: A: *I agree with the man. It's not important to remember names.*
> B: *I don't think so . . .*

> **Responses**
> I think so, too.
> I don't think so.

Warm up: Do you watch quiz shows? Which ones?

🎧 **Listen to *The Name Game*. Then complete the sentences.**

1. The first question is about _____.

   a. an athlete   b. a president   c. a king

2. The second question is about a _____.

   a. singer   b. writer   c. comedian

3. The third question is about _____.

   a. a dancer   b. a musician   c. an actor

Conversation Practice

GROUPS Choose a *nice* nickname for everyone in your group. Give a reason for the nickname. Tell the class the nickname. The class guesses your reason.

Example: *A: Donna's nickname is Blueberry.*
               B: Why?
               A: Her eyes are dark blue. They look like blueberries.

Listening Comprehension 2

Warm up: Are there rules about naming babies in your country? What are they?

🎧 **Listen to the rules for naming babies in Germany. Mark the statements true (T) or false (F).**

_____ 1. German citizens cannot give their children any name they want.

_____ 2. This rule began in 1975.

_____ 3. The German government doesn't want children to feel bad about their name.

_____ 4. In Germany, it's OK for parents to give a girl a boy's name.

_____ 5. Sometimes a judge decides about a name.

Now write true statements about naming a baby in your country. Use the sentences above as a model.

Some names have other meanings. Can you find eight English names? What are their meanings? Names can be across (→) or down (↓). (Check your answers on page 107.)

```
X   K   A   B   I   L   L   W

R   I   C   H   Y   U   M   I

O   J   R   O   B   I   N   L

S   O   F   R   A   Y   B   L

E   Y   M   A   R   K   E   X
```

HINTS:

1. opposite of poor

2. opposite of won't

3. a spot

4. steal

5. happiness

6. a flower

7. light from the sun

8. for example, a dollar

Unit 15 — Ounces and Other Measurements

Add the measurements to the pictures. (Check your answers on page 107.)

| 100 kph/60 mph | 100 grams/3.5 oz. | .5 liter/1 pt. 9 fl.oz | 67 kg/147.4 lbs. |

a. b. c. d.

kph= kilometers per hour
mph= miles per hour

fl oz= fluid ounces
kg= kilogram

lbs= pounds

Facts

Length	Mass	Volume
meters × 1.1 = yards kilometers × .6 = miles	grams × .035 = ounces kilograms × 2.2 = pounds	liters × 1.6 = quarts

A. GROUPS Try to complete the sentences.   <u>Were you right?</u>

1. The short form of *ounce* is oz. The short form of *pound* is _____.   _____

   a. pd   b. pnd   c. lb

2. Most of the world uses the metric system. Only the United States, Myanmar, and   _____
   _____ don't use it.

   a. Libya   b. Liberia   c. Lithuania

3. The metric system was created by French scientists in the _____.   _____

   a. 18th century   b. 19th century   c. 17th century

4. A meter is a little more than one _____.   _____

   a. inch   b. foot   c. yard

5. A liter is a _____ than a quart.   _____

   a. little more   b. little less   c. lot less

    Now listen and check your answers.

B. GROUPS

- Take turns saying the facts. Then close your books.
- How many facts can you remember? Say all the facts you remember.

Talk about Your Experience

A. PAIRS Answer the questions. Then ask your partner. Add information.

Example: A: *When do you use measurements?*
B: *When I cook. How about you?*
A: *When I drive.*

	YOU	YOUR PARTNER
• When do you use measurements?		
• What jobs use measurements?		
• What measurements do you know? (For example, I know my height.)		

Tell the class about your partner.

B. WHOLE CLASS Survey five students. Ask:

1. How much weight can you lift?

    a. between 5 and 10 kilograms   b. between 10 and 30 kilograms   c. more than 30 kilograms

2. How much water do you drink a day?

    a. .5 liter   b. 1–2 liters   c. more than 3 liters

3. How many kilometers do you walk each week?

    a. less than 20 kilometers   b. between 20 and 40 kilometers   c. more than 40 kilometers

Give Your Opinion

A. Listen to the opinion. Then listen to the responses.

> **The American system is hard.**

> I think so, too. I think the metric system is better.

> Really? I think the American system is easy.

B. PAIRS Do you agree with the man or the woman? Add your opinion.

Example: A: *I agree with the man. I think the American system is easy.*
I learned it in a couple of weeks.
B: *I think so, too . . .*

> **Responses**
> I think so, too.
> Really? I think . . .

Warm up: A prefix is a group of letters at the beginning of a word. It makes a new word.
If we add the prefix *un–*to the word *happy*, we make the word *unhappy*.
What does the prefix *un–*mean? Do you know other words that begin with *un–*? Do you know any other prefixes?

🎧 **Listen to a talk about prefixes that tell you a number. Then complete the chart.**

Prefix	Meaning	Example
bi		
	one one–hundredth (1/100)	
kilo		

Conversation Practice

GROUPS Guess the answers.

1. The distance around the earth is _____.
    a. about 40,000 km
    b. about 80,000 km
    c. about 140,000 km

2. The distance from the earth to the sun is _____.
    a. about 15 million km
    b. about 50 million km
    c. about 150 million km

3. The height of the Eiffel Tower is _____.
    a. about 300 meters
    b. about 1,300 meters
    c. about 130 meters

4. The weight of a baby elephant is _____.
    a. about 45 kg
    b. about 90 kg
    c. about 180 kg

(Check your answers on page 107.) Do any of the answers surprise you? Which ones?

Warm up: Do you have any questions about measurements?

🎧 **Listen to a radio show called, "Ask Any Question." Then complete the sentences.**

1. In London they spell *meter* and *liter* _____ and _____.

2. The short form for pound is lb. It comes from the word _____.

3. The *hand* is used to measure the _____ of a _____.

Check This Out

GROUPS Do you know what these temperatures measure?

1. 98.6 degrees Fahrenheit
2. 212 degrees Fahrenheit
3. 32 degrees Fahrenheit

$(°F − 32) \times 5/9 = °C$
$(°C \times 9/5) + 32 = °F$

(Check your answers on page 107.)

It's easy to take a photograph, but is it easy to take a good photograph?

Why or why not?

Do you like this photograph? Why or why not?

Alfred Steiglitz, *The City Across the River*

Facts

A. GROUPS Try to complete the sentences.

Were you right?

1. English-speaking photographers often say, "Say _____."

   a. please   b. freeze   c. cheese   _____

2. A *snapshot* is a _____.

   a. photo   b. gun   c. camera   _____

3. You need a _____ to take pictures in the dark.

   a. flashlight   b. flash   c. photo   _____

4. A portrait is a picture of _____.

   a. a person   b. a place   c. a thing   _____

5. A landscape is a picture of _____.

   a. a person   b. a city   c. nature   _____

6. People keep family photos in a photo _____.

   a. album   b. shop   c. case   _____

🎧 **Now listen and check your answers.**

B. GROUPS

- Take turns saying the facts. Then close your books.
- How many facts can you remember? Say all the facts you remember.

A. PAIRS Answer the questions. Then ask your partner. Add information.

Example: A: *Do you have a camera?*
   B: *Yes. I have three cameras: a digital camera, a 35mm camera, and a video camera.*
   I love to take pictures. How about you?

	YOU	YOUR PARTNER
• Do you have a camera? If so, what kind?		
• Do you usually take pictures of people? of cities? of nature? of things? Do you take black and white or color photos?		
• What makes a photo interesting to you?		
• Do you have many photo albums? Do you have any old photos? If so, who's in those photos? Are you carrying any photos with you now?		
• Do you have a video camera? When do you use it?		

Tell the class about your partner.

B. WHOLE CLASS Survey four students.
Ask: Who takes the most photos in your family?

Report the results to the class.

Give Your Opinion

A. Listen to the opinion. Then listen to the responses.

Many people take too many photos at parties.

I disagree. I think photos are the best way to remember a party.

I agree. I hate to pose for a photograph. I don't relax when someone is taking my picture.

B. PAIRS Do you agree with the man or the woman? Add your opinion.
Example: A: *I think the man is right. I think you should take lots of pictures at parties.*
   B: *I disagree . . .*

Responses
I agree.
I disagree.

Warm up: Many people call Alfred Steiglitz the "father of modern photography." Look at his photograph of *The City Across the River* on page 62. It's a photograph of New York City in the early 1900s. What three words describe the photo?

🎧 **Listen to a short biography of Steiglitz. Then complete the sentences.**

1. Steiglitz was born in _____ in _____.
                             (place)   (year)

2. His parents were _____.

3. He studied in both _____ and _____.

4. He became a photographer at the age of _____.

5. He opened a gallery on _____ in New York City.

6. He married the artist _____.

7. He died at the age of _____.

Conversation Practice

PAIRS Tell your partner about a photo you took.

What's in the photo? When did you take it? Where did you take it? Why did you take it? Do you like it? Why?

A. Look at these photos. How many differences can you find?

B. 🎧 Jack is looking at some photos. Listen to a conversation between Jack and his friend Pat. Look at the photos. Which photo are they talking about?

Check This Out

GROUPS Brett Weston took photographs of everyday things. What does this look like? (Check the answer on page 107.)

Unit *17* — Queens

Did you ever pretend to be a queen or a king?

Facts

A. GROUPS Guess which statements are true (T) and which statements are false (F).

<u>Your answer</u>   <u>Were you right?</u>

_____ 1.   Queen Victoria of England was queen for sixty-four years, from 1837 to 1901.   _____

_____ 2.   Cleopatra VII was the last queen of Greece. She ruled from 69 to 30 BCE.   _____

_____ 3.   The Queen of Sheba was married to King David.   _____

_____ 4.   Hawaii is the only state in the United States that had kings and queens.   _____

_____ 5.   The queen ant is the most important ant in the family.   _____

_____ 6.   The queen is the most powerful piece in a checkers game.   _____

🎧 **Now listen and check your answers. Change the false statements to true ones.**

B. GROUPS

- Take turns saying the facts. Then close your books.
- How many facts can you remember? Say all the facts you remember.

A. PAIRS Answer the questions. Then ask your partner. Add information.

Example: *A: Do you like to read about the lives of royalty?*
B: Yes, I do. I like to read magazine articles and biographies of them.

	YOU	YOUR PARTNER
• Do you like to read about the lives of royalty? What do you know about different kings, queens, princes, and princesses?		
• Have you visited any castles or palaces? Where? When?		
• As a child, did you ever pretend to be a king or a queen?		

Tell the class something about a king, queen, prince, or princess.

B. WHOLE CLASS Survey five students about royalty in England.

	Agree	**Disagree**
England does not need a king or queen.		

Report the results to the class.

Give Your Opinion

A. 🎧 **Listen to the opinion. Then listen to the responses.**

A queen has a very difficult job.

I agree.
She has to attend all sorts
of events and she doesn't
have any privacy.

I disagree.
I think most queens have
interesting and exciting lives.
After all, they're the queen.

B. PAIRS Do you agree with the man or the woman? Add your opinion.

Example: *A: I think the woman is right. A queen doesn't have*
the freedom of an ordinary person.
B: I disagree . . .

Responses
I agree.
I disagree.

Warm up: Do you know anything about Queen Liliuokalani?

 Listen to a talk about Queen Liliuokalani. Then answer the questions.

1. Where was she queen?
2. For how long was she the queen?
3. What did she write?
4. When was she born?
5. Where can you see her statue?

Conversation Practice

A. Study these words.

a king	a queen	a prince	a princess	a castle	a dragon	a dungeon
wicked	poor	rich	sad	happy	strong	smart	ugly	beautiful

B. PAIRS Make up a story with your partner. Use ten or more of the words in your story. Begin:

Once upon a time there was a . . .

Then read your story to the class.

Warm up: Would you like to travel on a ship like the one in the photo?

🎧 **Listen to an ad for a cruise on the *Queen Mary 2*. Check (✓) the things the ship offers.**

_____ swimming pools

_____ golf

_____ shops

_____ a spa

_____ an aquarium

_____ a planetarium

_____ British nannies

_____ British candies

Check This Out

GROUPS Can you match the palace with the country? (Check your answers on page 107.)

a.

b.

c.

d.

| France | Japan | England | Thailand |

Would you like to live in a palace? Why or why not?

Unit 18   "Red" Idioms

**Does your town roll out the red carpet *for anyone? For who?*

Facts

A. GROUPS Try to complete the sentences.   <u>Were you right?</u>

1. She *saw red* when he asked for more money. She was _____.   _____

   a. happy   b. angry   c. sad

2. Her jewelry was in his pocket. They caught him *red-handed*. He was _____.   _____

   a. doing something illegal   b. cooking something   c. painting

3. He took the *red-eye* from San Francisco to New York. He took a _____.   _____

   a. sick person   b. colorblind person   c. night flight

4. The company is *in the red*. The company _____.   _____

   a. is doing well   b. is not doing well   c. is closing

5. The Yankees were *red hot* last night. They _____ the game 11–0.   _____

   a. won   b. lost   c. tied

  🎧 **Now listen and check your answers.**

B. GROUPS

- Take turns saying the facts. Then close your books.
- How many facts can you remember? Say all the facts you remember.

A. PAIRS Answer the questions. Then ask your partner. Add information.

> *Example*: *A: Do you like the color red?*
> *B: Red's OK. Sometimes I wear red socks or a red scarf. How about you? Do you like red?*
> *A: I love red. I have lots of red things. I have two red sweaters and a red jacket. My carpet is red, too.*

	YOU	YOUR PARTNER
• Do you like red? Do you have a lot of red clothes? Do you have any red things in your house? • When you think of red, what do you think of? fire? blood? love? excitement?		

Do you and your partner think of the same things when you think of red?

B. WHOLE CLASS Discuss these questions.

1. To *see red* means to be angry. When you're angry, what color do you see?
2. To *roll out the red carpet* is to treat someone like a king or queen. Is red a royal color in your country?

Give Your Opinion

A. 🎧 Listen to the opinion. Then listen to the responses.

> Red is a very popular color among teenagers.

I think so, too. Many teens buy red cars.

Really? I think most teens prefer black. They always wear black.

B. PAIRS Do you agree with the man or the woman? Add your opinion.

> *Example*: *A: I agree with the woman. Everyone I know wears black.*
> *B: Really? I think . . .*

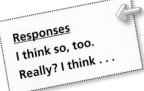

Responses
I think so, too.
Really? I think . . .

Warm up: You want to get a driver's license. You need to answer a lot of questions and fill out a lot of forms. Your friend says, "I know the head of the license department. I'll help you *cut through the red tape.*" What does *cut through the red tape* mean? Can you guess where the idiom comes from?

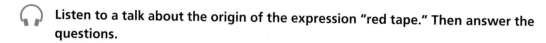 **Listen to a talk about the origin of the expression "red tape." Then answer the questions.**

1. Who used red tape in the past?
2. Why did they use it?
3. When did people first use the idiom?
4. In what country did they use this expression?

Conversation Practice

A. GROUPS Write the letter of the idiom next to the situation. (Check your answers on page 107.)

a. It was a red-letter day for him.	c. He took the red-eye.
b. We rolled out the red carpet for her.	d. He was caught red-handed.

_____ 1. They found the money in his briefcase.

_____ 2. He won the state championship in tennis.

_____ 3. His plane left Seattle at 10 p.m. It arrived in New York at 7 a.m.

_____ 4. The queen came to our town.

B. GROUPS With your group, write a new situation. Ask the class for the correct idiom from the ones in the box.

Listening Comprehension 2

Warm up: What color do you prefer, red or blue? Why?

Listen to a psychologist talk about the colors red and blue. Then read the sentences. Write R for red or B for blue next to the correct sentence.

_____ 1. This color makes people breathe faster.

_____ 2. This color relaxes people.

_____ 3. This color grabs people's attention.

_____ 4. This color makes people feel like fighting.

_____ 5. This color makes people work harder.

GROUPS **Look at the pictures. Complete the sentences with the correct colors. One color will be used twice.** (Check your answers on page 107.)

blue	black	green	rose

1. He rarely calls. He calls once in a _____ moon.

2. His girlfriend left him. He feels _____.

3. He's the only one in his family who gets in trouble. He's the _____ sheep of the family.

4. Everything always looks better to him than it really is. He sees everything with _____-colored glasses.

5. When his neighbor built a swimming pool, he was _____ with envy.

Unit 19 Strange and Unusual Things

Look at the photo. What do you see?

Guess where it was taken.
(Check your answer on page 107.)

Facts

A. GROUPS Try to complete the sentences.

<u>**Were you right?**</u>

1. It's impossible for people to lick their _____.

   a. toes   b. elbows   c. knees   _____

2. Women blink _____ as men.

   a. nearly twice as often   b. half as often   c. about the same   _____

3. More people use _____ toothbrushes than red ones.

   a. yellow   b. white   c. blue   _____

4. A _____ can live several weeks with its head cut off.

   a. cockroach   b. ant   c. mouse   _____

5. You're born with about 300 bones. When you are an adult you have _____ bones.   _____

   a. 406   b. 306   c. 206

6. You want to say something surprising. You begin, "_____"…   _____

   a. "Believe it or not"   b. "Believe me"   c. "I believe"

🎧 **Now listen and check your answers.**

B. GROUPS
- Take turns saying the facts. Then close your books.
- How many facts can you remember? Say all the facts you remember.

A. PAIRS Answer the questions. Then ask your partner. Add information.

Example: A: *Can you remember a strange event in your life or in the life of someone you know?*
B: *Yes. My aunt told me about a strange dream.*

	YOU	YOUR PARTNER
• Can you remember a strange event in your life or in the life of someone you know? Tell about the event. • What happened? When did it happen? • Where did it happen?		

Tell the class about your experience.

Example: *Last year my aunt had a dream. In it she saw my uncle on an elephant. The next week my uncle won a trip to Thailand.*

B. WHOLE CLASS Discuss this question:

Which event was the strangest?

Give Your Opinion

A. 🎧 Listen to the opinion. Then listen to the responses.

> It's fun to try unusual food.

I agree. Last month I tried rattlesnake. It was good.

I disagree. I like to eat the same things every day.

B. PAIRS Do you agree with the man or the woman? Add your opinion.

Example: A: *I agree with the man. I like to try new food.*
B: *I agree . . .*

Responses
I agree.
I disagree.

Some U.S. cities and states have very unusual laws. These laws are old, and no one really follows them. Read the chart. Then listen to the laws and complete the chart.

| Missouri | Corpus Christie, Texas | Cleveland, Ohio | Massachusetts |
| North Carolina | Virginia | Tennessee |

Place	Law
	A man can't shave without a permit.
	You can't raise alligators in your home.
	You can't leave chewing gum in public places.
	Chickens must lay their eggs between 8:00 a.m. and 4:00 p.m.
	Rabbits can't race down the street.
	You can't put tomatoes in clam chowder.
	You can't drive while sleeping.

Conversation Practice

GROUPS Read about Brandon. Then answer the questions.

Brandon was born with a brain tumor.* The doctors said it was very bad. Sometimes these tumors go away before a baby's first birthday. This one didn't. Brandon still had the tumor at two. Doctors decided to remove it. Just before the operation, the tumor went away. Now Brandon is a healthy little boy.

How do you explain this?
Do you know any other medical surprises? Tell your group. Begin, "Can you believe this?"

* abnormal growth

Warm up: The *Guinness Book of World Records* is one of the most popular books in the world. It tells about people or things that "set records." For example, you can read about the biggest cookie, the longest river, or the fattest king. Did you ever think about "setting a record"? How?

 Listen to the information from the *Guinness Book of World Records*. Then answer the questions.

1. What's beautiful in Myanmar?
2. What do women wear around their necks in Myanmar?
3. What happened to Hoo Sateow after he got a haircut?
4. How long is Hoo Sateow's hair?

Check This Out

WHOLE CLASS How many of your classmates believe in life on other planets? Why or why not?

Unit 20 Tai Chi and Other Martial Arts

What do you know about martial arts? Do you know where these are from?
(Check your answers on page 107.)

hapkido	capoeira	tai chi	karate

| Brazil | Japan | Korea | China |

Facts

A. GROUPS Try to complete the sentences.   **Were you right?**

1. Tai chi helps _____ .   _____

   a. only the mind   b. only the body   c. both the mind and body

2. Judo comes from Japan. It means "empty _____."   _____

   a. foot   b. hand   c. mind

3. Tae kwon do comes from Korea. It is famous for _____ .   _____

   a. high kicks   b. high jumps   c. low bows

4. Moves of the tiger, crane, leopard, snake, and dragon are a part of _____ .   _____

   a. kung fu   b. tai chi   c. Thai boxing

5. The first _____ competition at the Olympic Games was in 1964.   _____

   a. tai chi   b. judo   c. hapkido

 Now listen and check your answers.

B. GROUPS

- Take turns saying the facts. Then close your books.
- How many facts can you remember? Say all the facts you remember.

A. PAIRS Answer the questions. Then ask your partner. Add information.

Example: A: *Can you do any of the martial arts?*
            B: *Not really. I took a karate class once, but I never finished it.*

	YOU	YOUR PARTNER
• Can you do any of the martial arts? Which ones? • What do you do to relax? • I take a walk. • I exercise. • I sleep. • I do yoga or tai chi. • I watch TV. • I visit a friend. • I drink some tea. • I get a massage. • I take a hot bath.		

Tell the class how you and your partner relax.

B. WHOLE CLASS
How are the martial arts different from sports like soccer or basketball?

Give Your Opinion

A. 🎧 **Listen to the opinion. Then listen to the responses.**

> It's more fun to watch team sports than martial arts.

> I agree. It's more exciting.

> I disagree. I like both. It's exciting to watch a great tae kwon do expert. It's also exciting to watch a great soccer match.

B. PAIRS Do you agree with the man or the woman? Add your opinion.

Example: A: *I agree with the man. I prefer to watch team sports.*
            B: *I disagree . . .*

Responses
I agree.
I disagree.

Warm up: Would you like to take a tai chi class? Why or why not? Would you prefer to take a different martial arts class?

 Listen to a radio ad for tai chi classes. Then answer the questions.

1. When do the classes begin?
2. Who can go?
3. What time are the classes?
4. What days are they?
5. Where are they?
6. What is the number for more information?

Conversation Practice

GROUPS Teach your group a martial arts step or a dance step, or lead them in some excercise. Use some of the words below.

stand	put	bend	move	shake	lift	lower	swing	reach
arm	leg	hand	foot	head	eyes	shoulders		touch

Example: Everyone please stand.
　　　　　　　Put your arms in the air.
　　　　　　　Bend your elbows.
　　　　　　　Shake your hands.
　　　　　　　Now reach to the floor.
　　　　　　　Swing your arms.
　　　　　　　Stand.
　　　　　　　Shake your right leg.
　　　　　　　Shake your left leg.
　　　　　　　Close your eyes.
　　　　　　　Open your eyes.

A woman calls about tai chi classes. Listen to the telephone conversation. Answer the woman's questions.

1. What do I wear to class?

   a. loose clothes   b. a robe   c. jeans

2. Do I need special shoes?

   a. Heels are best.   b. The Chinese slipper is best.   c. Boots are best.

3. Do people use tai chi for self-defense?

   a. No, never.   b. Yes, they do.   c. Not very often.

4. Why is tai chi so popular?

   a. It helps you relax.   b. It helps you lose weight.   c. It helps you gain weight.

5. Who can do tai chi?

   a. anyone   b. anyone between the ages of twelve and forty   c. anyone between the ages of sixteen and sixty

Check This Out

GROUPS

A balance of *yin* and *yang* is a part of tai chi. *Yin* is the female, and *yang* is the male.

What do you know about *yin* and *yang*?

Look at my family tree. Write the missing relationships: my brother, my uncle, my aunt, my grandmother, my grandfather.

Facts

A. GROUPS **Try to complete the sentences.**

Were you right?

1. Your great-uncle is _____ .

   a. the oldest brother of your mother or father
   b. a brother of your grandmother or grandfather
   c. your oldest niece or nephew

   _____

2. The U.S. government is sometimes called Uncle _____ .

   a. Bob
   b. Charlie
   c. Sam

   _____

3. Your uncle's wife is your _____ .

   a. aunt
   b. sister
   c. in-law

   _____

4. *Uncle* _____ *Cabin* is a book by Harriet Beecher Stowe.

   a. *Tom's*
   b. *Dan's*
   c. *Ted's*

   _____

5. You say "I'll be a monkey's uncle" when you are _____ to hear something.

   a. happy
   b. angry
   c. surprised

   _____

   Now listen and check your answers.

B. GROUPS

- Take turns saying the facts. Then close your books.
- How many facts can you remember? Say all the facts you remember.

Talk about Your Experience

A. PAIRS Answer the questions. Then ask your partner. Add information.

Example: A: *How many uncles do you have?*
B: *I have six uncles. They live all over the world. Two live in the United States, two live in Spain, one lives in Thailand, and one lives in Colombia.*

	YOU	YOUR PARTNER
• How many uncles do you have? • How often do you see your uncles? • How old is your oldest uncle? How old is your youngest uncle? • In some cultures a wife marries her husband's brother when her husband dies. What do you think of that custom?		

Tell the class about your partner's uncles.

Example: *My partner has two uncles. One uncle is an architect. He built many buildings in this city.*

B. WHOLE CLASS Survey five students.

Ask:
How many uncles do you have? How old are they?
Who has the most uncles? the fewest? the oldest? the youngest?

Report the results to the class.

Give Your Opinion

A. 🎧 **Listen to the opinion. Then listen to the responses.**

> **Blood is thicker than water. Relatives are more important than friends.**

> I think so, too. A family has to stay together. A family always comes first.

> I don't think so. You can choose your friends. You can't choose your family.

B. PAIRS Do you agree with the man or the woman? Add your opinion.

Example: A: *I agree with the woman. I like my friends more than I like some of my relatives.*
B: *I think so, too . . .*

> **Responses**
> I think so, too.
> I don't think so.

Warm up: How many uncles does your mother have?

 Listen to someone talk about his family. Take notes.
How many uncles does the speaker have?

(Check your answer on page 107.)

Conversation Practice

A. PAIRS Complete the list of male and female relatives. Which two relatives can be either male or female? (Check your answers on page 107.)

Male	Female
brother	aunt

- aunt
- brother
- cousin
- father
- grandfather
- grandmother
- mother
- nephew
- niece
- parent
- sister
- uncle

B. GROUPS Tell about a special relative in your family.
Who is it? Why is this person special?

Jon is getting married.

Jon? Well, I'll be a monkey's uncle. I thought Jon was never going to marry.

Warm up: When something is hard to believe, we say *I'll be a monkey's uncle*. Do you know where the idiom comes from?

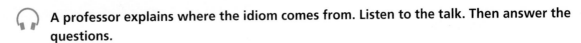 A professor explains where the idiom comes from. Listen to the talk. Then answer the questions.

1. When was the expression *I'll be a monkey's uncle* first used?
2. What was Charles Darwin's profession?
3. What did the book say about humans, apes, and monkeys?
4. Did everyone like the idea of the book?

Check This Out

GROUPS What's good about a large family?

INSURANCE SALESMAN OF THE YEAR

www.CartoonStock.com

"......And finally I'd like to thank my 5 brothers, 4 sisters, 3 uncles, 2 aunts, 23 nephews and nieces and 37 cousins."

Unit 22 Vending Machines

What was the last thing you bought from a vending machine?

When did you buy it?

Facts

A. GROUPS Try to complete the sentences.

<u>**Were you right?**</u>

1. In 1880 in England, the first vending machine sold _____.

   a. soda   b. stamps   c. postcards

   _____

2. For over sixty years, Horn and Hardart was a cafeteria chain in the United States. The food was behind glass doors. To get the food, you put money in an opening. The restaurant opened in _____.

   a. 1902   b. 1922   c. 1942

   _____

3. You need _____ for some vending machines.

   a. identification   b. exact change   c. exact time

   _____

4. Vending machines have an opening for coins. The opening is called a _____.

   a. slot   b. lot   c. spot

   _____

5. _____ has the largest variety of vending machines.

   a. China   b. Japan   c. The United States

   _____

   🎧 **Now listen and check your answers.**

B. GROUPS

- Take turns saying the facts. Then close your books.
- How many facts can you remember? Say all the facts you remember.

A. PAIRS Answer the questions. Then ask your partner. Add information.

Example: *A: What do you buy from vending machines?*
            B: Candy and soda. I also buy stamps, train tickets, and tennis balls.

	YOU	YOUR PARTNER
• Do you often buy things from vending machines?		
• What do you buy?		
• What do you like about vending machines? What don't you like?		
• A U.S. company (Maytag) makes vending machines for the home. They can hold sixty-six cans of soda. They come in different colors. Would you like a vending machine for your home? Why or why not?		

Would you and your partner both like a vending machine in your home? Why or why not?

B. WHOLE CLASS
What things do students in your class buy from vending machines? Write a list on the board.

Give Your Opinion

A. Listen to the opinion. Then listen to the responses.

> **Food from vending machines is never very good.**

> I agree. Food from vending machines never tastes fresh.

> I don't think so. I buy delicious candy from vending machines all the time.

B. PAIRS Do you agree with the man or the woman? Add your opinion.

Example: *A: I think the woman is right. I buy lots of food from vending*
            machines. Most of the time it's delicious.
            B: I don't think so . . .

Responses
I agree.
I don't think so.

Listening Comprehension 1

Warm up: What unusual things can you buy from vending machines?

🎧 Vending machines sell all sorts of things. Listen to some of the things you can buy. Check (✓) the things you hear about in this talk.

_____ 1. blue birds   _____ 6. worms

_____ 2. blue jeans   _____ 7. your fortune

_____ 3. shrimp   _____ 8. a phone

_____ 4. cats   _____ 9. art

_____ 5. frogs   _____ 10. music

Conversation Practice

WHOLE CLASS What do you think? Read the statements and give your opinions to the class.

a. There will be fewer vending machines in our city in the future.

b. There will be more vending machines in our city in the future.

c. Vending machines will take jobs away from people.

d. Vending machines will be harder to use in the future.

Listening Comprehension 2

Warm up: You want to buy a drink from a vending machine. You don't have money. How do you get the drink?

🎧 An article in the *Financial News* in October 2003 discusses the way people in South Korea can buy things without money. Listen to the article. Then complete the sentences.

1. Kim Won-jung paid for a drink from _____ using her cell phone.

   a. a friend   b. a café   c. a vending machine

2. In South Korea telecom companies, credit card companies, and _____ are working together.

   a. banks   b. universities   c. the government

3. There are 48 million people in Korea and _____ million cell phone users.

   a. 13.2   b. 33.2   c. 3.2

4. Today people in South Korea use cell phones to surf the Internet, transfer money, play the lottery, buy movie tickets, and _____.

   a. take pictures   b. fix computers   c. drive cars

A. GROUPS Do you often see Out of Order signs on vending machines?

B. GROUPS How many new words can you make from the letters in the phrase *out of order*?

Unit 23 Weddings

What is the best month to marry? Why?
What is the best age to marry? Why?

Facts

A. GROUPS Try to complete the sentences.

Were you right?

1. In a traditional Western wedding, the bride wears a white wedding _____ . _____
   a. gown   b. crown   c. frown

2. The man getting married is called the _____ . _____
   a. gloom   b. groom   c. broom

3. You think two people will marry. You say, "I hear wedding _____." _____
   a. bells   b. songs   c. words

4. At traditional weddings in _____, the groom gives his bride thirteen gold coins. _____
   a. Kenya   b. India   c. Mexico

5. At traditional weddings in _____, someone paints the bride's hands. _____
   a. Korea   b. Germany   c. India

6. After a wedding, the couple often goes on a _____. _____
   a. honeymoon   b. magic carpet   c. moon walk

🎧 **Now listen and check your answers.**

B. GROUPS

- Take turns saying the facts. Then close your books.
- How many facts can you remember? Say all the facts you remember.

Talk about Your Experience

A. PAIRS Answer the questions. Then ask your partner. Add information.

Example: A: *Do you prefer big weddings or small ones?*
B: *I usually prefer small ones. You meet more people and really talk to them.*

	YOU	YOUR PARTNER
• Do you prefer big weddings or small ones?		
• What wedding traditions do you like? Why? What traditions do you dislike? Why?		
• Some people marry in secret. They do not tell anyone in advance. They "elope." Do you know anyone who eloped?		
• Do you think women are more excited about weddings than men? Why?		

Tell the class about the kind of wedding you and your partner like.

B. WHOLE CLASS Survey five students.

Ask: Is money the best wedding gift?

Report the results to the class.

Give Your Opinion

A. 🎧 Listen to the opinion. Then listen to the responses.

When you marry, it's important to like the person's family.

I agree. It's true. You are a part of the whole family—the brothers, sisters, parents, and grandparents.

I disagree. It's not important to like the person's family. Some people move away and have their own lives.

B. PAIRS Do you agree with the man or the woman? Add your opinion.

Example: A: *I agree with the woman. You don't marry the person's family. You marry the person.*
B: *I disagree . . .*

Responses
I agree.
I disagree.

Pranee and Carmen are classmates in an ESL class. Listen to them talk about a wedding custom in Thailand. Then answer the questions.

1. Who got married?

2. What is Khan Mark?

3. What do the friends and relatives of the groom do during Khan Mark?

Conversation Practice

GROUPS Tell about a wedding you attended.

- Where was it?

- When was it?

- Who got married?

- How do you know the people?

- How many people attended the wedding?

- How long was the wedding?

- What was traditional about this wedding?

- What was different about this wedding?

🎧 A bridal shower is a party for the woman getting married. A friend or relative gives the party. Listen to the telephone conversation. Then complete the invitation.

Please join us
for
A Bridal Shower

The party is on _____.

The party is at _____.

The party is for _____.

Please bring a gift to use in the _____.

Please bring a _____, too.

Check This Out

"You want only happiness, Douglas. I want wealth, power, fame, and happiness."

GROUPS Why do people marry?

Unit 24 X + 4 = ?

Match the puzzles with their meanings.

Made in China.	History, history, history
One in a million.	E *more more more more*
Repeat after me.	*me* **REPEAT**
Ready for more?	Millio1n
History repeats itself.	ChiMADEna

Do you like puzzles? Why or why not?

Facts

$$(2 (3X-1) = 3 (X+5) -4)$$

A. GROUPS Try to complete the sentences.   Were you right?

1. A _____ is a question with a funny answer.   _____
   a. middle   b. riddle   c. fiddle

2. Someone finds the answer to a problem. The person says, "I've _____ it."   _____
   a. had   b. got   c. made

3. Some people can think of new ways to do things. We say they think "outside the _____."   _____
   a. box   b. brain   c. border

4. A picture with many pieces is a _____ puzzle.   _____
   a. see-saw   b. so-so   c. jigsaw

5. In a crossword puzzle you try to find the correct _____.   _____
   a. number   b. word   c. rule

   🎧 **Now listen and check your answers.**

B. GROUPS

- Take turns saying the facts. Then close your books.
- How many facts can you remember? Say all the facts you remember.

Talk about Your Experience

A. PAIRS Answer the questions. Then ask your partner. Add information.

Example: A: *Do you like puzzles?*

               B: *Some. I really like crossword puzzles.*

	YOU	YOUR PARTNER

• Do you like puzzles? What kind do you like?
   • number puzzles
   • word puzzles
   • jigsaw puzzles
   • crossword puzzles
• When do you do puzzles?
• Do you like to work alone or with others?		

Tell the class one thing about your partner.

B. WHOLE CLASS Answer the questions. Then survey four students. Count the number of men and women who answer *yes* and *no* for each question.

	YOU		MEN		WOMEN	
	Yes	No	Yes	No	Yes	No
I like number puzzles.						
I like word puzzles.						
I'm good at number puzzles.						
I'm good at word puzzles.						

Give Your Opinion

A. 🎧 **Listen to the opinion. Then listen to the responses.**

> **People learn a lot from puzzles.**

I agree. You need to think when you do a puzzle.

I disagree. Puzzles are fun, but you usually don't learn anything.

B. PAIRS Do you agree with the man or the woman? Add your opinion.

Example: A: *I think the man is right. I think puzzles teach you to think more clearly.*

               B: *I disagree . . .*

Responses

I agree.

I disagree.

$X + Y = ?$ 95

Warm up: Many children like riddles. Read the riddle. Do you think it's funny?

A: A dog is running and wearing a coat on a hot summer day. What do you call this dog?

B: I don't know.

A: A hotdog.

🎧 **Listen to these riddles. Then complete the sentences.**

1. A: Why did the frog eat the lamp?

   B: He wanted a _____.

2. A: What side of a rabbit has the most fur?

   B: The _____.

3. A: How far can you walk into a forest?

   B: _____. Then you're walking *out* of the forest.

Conversation Practice   Information Gap

Student A, turn to page 106. Student B, turn to page 108.

Warm up: Match the words and their opposites.

1. more than   a. lighter
2. heavier   b. less than

 Now listen to someone talk about the weight of five dogs: Jam, Jelly, Copper, Brandy, and Pumpkin.
List the dogs in order of their weight. Start with the heaviest.
(Check your answers on page 107.)

HINT: Write each name on a separate card.

1.

2.

3.

4.

5. *Jelly*

Check This Out

GROUPS Can you solve this puzzle? Move two matches to form four equal squares.

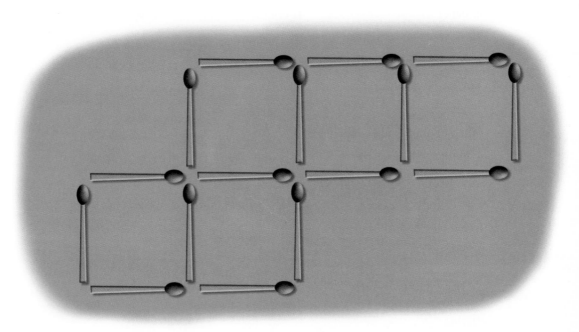

Where are these from? (Check your answers on page 107.)

Dollar   Yen   Peso   Pound

Facts

A. GROUPS Try to complete the sentences.

Were you right?

1. A U.S. dollar bill is 75% _____.

   a. paper   b. cotton   c. silk   _____

2. "Can you change a dollar?" means you want _____.

   a. coins for the dollar   b. a different dollar   c. a clean dollar   _____

3. You have some yen. You want dollars. You ask, "What's the rate of _____?"   _____

   a. change   b. exchange   c. transfer

4. Many countries in Europe use the _____.   _____

   a. mark   b. pound   c. euro

5. The first person to collect coins was _____.   _____

   a. Alexander the Great   b. Augustus Caesar   c. King Louis X

6. In the past people used cattle, tea, and _____ as money.   _____

   a. leaves   b. bread   c. shells

🎧 **Now listen and check your answers.**

B. GROUPS

- Take turns saying the facts. Then close your books.
- How many facts can you remember? Say all the facts you remember.

Talk about Your Experience

A. PAIRS Answer the questions. Then ask your partner. Add information.

> **Example:** A: *Do you have coins from different countries?*
> B: *Yes, I do. When I travel, I always keep a few coins. I have coins from Peru, Mexico, and the United States.*

	YOU	YOUR PARTNER
• Do you have coins from different countries? From where?		
• Do you collect coins?		
• Did you ever buy a coin? Did you ever sell a coin?		
• Do you have any interesting coins on you now?		

Tell the class about a coin you or your partner have.

B. WHOLE CLASS Discuss these questions.

1. Do you prefer to use credit cards, checks, or cash? Why?
2. Are credit cards a problem for anyone you know? Why?

Give Your Opinion

A. 🎧 Listen to the opinion. Then listen to the responses.

> **Money doesn't buy happiness.**

> I agree. There are more important things in life, like friends, family, and health.

> I disagree. Money can't buy health, but it can buy all the other things that make people happy.

B. PAIRS Do you agree with the man or the woman? Add your opinion.

> **Example:** A: *I agree with the woman. Money can buy almost everything.*
> B: *I disagree . . .*

> Responses
> I agree.
> I disagree.

Listening Comprehension 1

🎧 **A man is at the airport. He wants to change money. Listen to the conversations. Then answer the questions.**

1. Where can the man change money?
2. How much money does the man want to change?
3. Into what currency does he want to change it?
4. Does the woman give the man the money?

Conversation Practice

A. GROUPS Try and match the currency and the country. Choose from the words in the box. (Check your answers on page 107.)

baht	won	real	dinar	yuan	riyal	zloty	rupee

1. Brazil _____
2. China _____
3. India _____
4. Jordan _____
5. Poland _____
6. Saudi Arabia _____
7. South Korea _____
8. Thailand _____

B. WHOLE CLASS Take out a bill. Say as many things as you can about it.

Example: *This is a U.S. five-dollar bill. One side has a picture of a man. The man's name is Abraham Lincoln. He was a U.S. President.*

Listening Comprehension 2

🎧 **Listen to a radio interview with a coin collector. Mark the statements true (T) or false (F). Change the false statements to true ones.**

_____ 1. Mr. Silver is a new coin collector.

_____ 2. Old coins are always more valuable than new coins.

_____ 3. Location is very important when you buy a coin.

_____ 4. The condition of a coin is most important.

_____ 5. It's a good idea to clean a coin.

GROUPS Will coins and paper money disappear in the future?

American English	British English
traveler	traveller
check	cheque

What does the little boy think?

What do you think of this cartoon?

SIPRESS

*"He didn't do anything, Gregory.
This is a zoo."*

Facts

A. GROUPS Try to complete the sentences.

<u>**Were you right?**</u>

1. More than 4,500 years ago, there were zoos in _____.   _____
   a. Greece   b. China   c. Egypt

2. The first zoos were built for _____.   _____
   a. kings and queens   b. children   c. older people

3. Today, the largest zoo in the world is in _____.   _____
   a. San Diego   b. Berlin   c. Bangkok

4. Most zoos today don't keep animals in _____.   _____
   a. prisons   b. cages   c. caves

5. An animal doctor is called a _____.   _____
   a. veterinarian   b. vegetarian   c. dentist

6. Virginia McKenna was the star of a movie about animals called _____.   _____
   a. *Animal House*   b. *Born Free*   c. *The Lion King*

🎧 **Now listen and check your answers.**

B. GROUPS

- Take turns saying the facts. Then close your books.
- How many facts can you remember? Say all the facts you remember.

Talk about Your Experience

A. PAIRS Answer the questions. Then ask your partner. Add information.

Example: A: *Do you own a pet?*
   B: *Yes, I do. I have a dog. It's a hunting dog.*

	YOU	YOUR PARTNER
• Do you like to visit zoos? Do you have a favorite zoo? Where is it? What animals do you like to look at? Why?		
• Do you own a pet? If so, what kind? What's the name of your pet? Where does it live? If not, do you want a pet? What kind? Why or why not?		

Tell the class about a pet.

B. WHOLE CLASS Look at the photo. Discuss the following questions.

There's a saying: A *leopard can't change its spots.*

What does it mean? Do you agree?
Do you know sayings that include animals?
What are they? Write them on the board. What do they mean?

Give Your Opinion

A. 🎧 Listen to the opinion. Then listen to the responses.

> **Zoos are a great place to learn about animals.**

I think so, too.
You can see animals from all over the world and learn a lot from watching them.

I don't think so.
I think zoos are terrible.
Even the best zoos are bad for the animals.

B. PAIRS Do you agree with the man or the woman? Add your opinion.
Example: A: *I think the man is right. You can learn a lot from looking*
           at animals.
          B: *I think so, too . . .*

> **Responses**
> I think so, too.
> I don't think so.

Listening Comprehension 1

 Listen to a talk about zoos.

1. Circle the countries you hear about in this talk.

India	Egypt	China	Germany	Mexico	Singapore	Greece	Austria

2. Circle the times you hear about in this talk.

- 5,400 years ago
- 4,500 years ago
- 3,000 years ago
- 1,500 years ago
- 8th century

- 18th century
- From the 400s to the 700s
- From the 1400s to the 1700s
- Today

Conversation Practice

A. GROUPS Name one animal for each letter of the alphabet. The group with the most animals wins.

B. WHOLE CLASS A student tells four facts about an animal. The class guesses the animal.

Example: *A: It lives in caves. It's big. It's black, brown, or white. It sleeps during the winter.*
           B: Is it a bear?
           A: Yes, it is.

Listening Comprehension 2

 Listen to a talk about zoos. Then complete the chart.

Number of zoos today	
Largest zoo	
Second largest zoo	
Oldest public zoo	
First children's zoo	

Balance—The Key to a Good Life

GROUPS What does this mean?

Design a poster with an animal. Show it to your class.

Unit 1

Student A, ask your partner questions. Then complete the chart.

Example: *What kind of movie is* Meet Mr. Muffin?
Who's in Men at War?

Name of Movie	Kind of Movie	Actors	Next Show	Theater
Star Trip	Science fiction	Jonathan Lam	6:00 p.m.	Cineplex
Love Forever	Romance	Dahlia Lopez	6:30 p.m.	Lowes
Meet Mr. Muffin				
Men at War				

Unit 4

A. Today most diamonds come from South Africa. Find out about other stones and metals. Ask your partner questions to complete the chart. Then look at the chart, and answer your partner's questions.

Example: A: *Where can I buy gold?*
B: *You can buy gold in Thailand.*

Stone or Metal		Country
emeralds		Colombia
gold		
jade		Taiwan
lapiz		
opals		Australia
pearls		
silver		Mexico
turquoise		

B. Now talk to your partner about the different stones and metals. What do you know about them?

Unit 24

1. Student B will read you a riddle. Try to solve it. Look at the picture to help you. If you can't solve it, say, "Can I have a hint?"

2. Now read this riddle to Student B.

Two students are sitting on opposite sides of the same desk. There is nothing between them but the desk. They can't see each other. Why?

If your partner can't solve it, give this hint:
How were the students sitting?
Answer to Student B's riddle:
They were sitting back to back.

Answers to Selected Exercises

Unit 1   Opener

Jennifer Lopez as a teenager.

Unit 4   Check This Out

1. b   2. a   3. a

Unit 5   Conversation Practice

2. a. In case of fire, stay low.
3. a. In case of earthquake, hide under something heavy.
4. b. In case of earthquake, don't stand near a window.

Unit 7   Opener

a. I don't believe you.
b. I'm angry.

Unit 7   Listening Comprehension 1

a smile

Unit 7   Conversation Practice

1. head	5. mouth	9. finger
2. eyebrow	6. arm	10. leg
3. eye	7. hand	11. foot
4. nose	8. shoulder	

Unit 7   Check This Out

1. b   2. c   3. d   4. a

Unit 13   Opener

a. Liberia   b. Peru   c. Nigeria   d. Bali

Unit 14   Opener

Shaq= Shaquille O'Neal
Guga= Gustavo Kuerten
Magic= Earvin Johnson
Godzilla= Hideki Matsui

Unit 14   Check This Out

1. Rich	3. Mark	5. Joy	7. Ray
2. Will	4. Rob	6. Rose	8. Bill

Unit 15   Opener

a. 67 kg/147.4 lbs.
b. .5 liter/1 pt. 9 fl. oz.
c. 100 kph/60 mph
d. 100 grams/3.5 oz.

Unit 15   Conversation Practice

1. a. (24,900 miles)   3. a. (330 yards)
2. c. (93 million miles)   4. b. (200 pounds)

Unit 15   Check This Out

1. normal body temperature
2. boiling point of water
3. freezing point of water

Unit 16   Check This Out

a leaf

Unit 17   Check This Out

a. Thailand   b. England   c. France   d. Japan

Unit 18   Conversation Practice

1. d   2. a   3. c   4. b

Unit 18   Check This Out

1. blue   2. blue   3. black   4. rose   5. green

Unit 19   Opener

It's a photo of Mars. It was taken by Viking 1 in 1976. It looks like a woman buried in the sand.

Unit 20   Opener

hapkido: Korea   tai chi: China
capoeira: Brazil   karate: Japan

Unit 21   Listening Comprehension 1

The speaker has six uncles.

Unit 21   Conversation Practice

cousin, parent

Unit 24   Listening Comprehension 2

1. Jam	3. Copper	5. Jelly
2. Pumpkin	4. Brandy	

Unit 25   Opener

dollar: United States   peso: Mexico
yen: Japan   pound: Britain

Unit 25   Conversation Practice

1. real	3. rupee	5. zloty	7. won
2. yuan	4. dinar	6. riyal	8. baht

Unit 1

Student B, ask your partner questions. Then complete the chart.

Example: *What kind of movie is* Star Trip?
                    Who's in Love Forever?

Name of Movie	Kind of Movie	Actors	Next Show	Theater
Star Trip				
Love Forever				
Meet Mr. Muffin	Comedy	Scott Rusell Dan Phillips	6:30 p.m.	Movieplex
Men at War	Action	Harris Wall Jan Muraoka	6:45 p.m.	Movieplex

Unit 4

A. Today most diamonds come from South Africa. Find out about other stones and metals. Ask your partner questions to complete the chart. Then look at the chart, and answer your partner's questions.

Example: *A: Where can I buy emeralds?*
                    B: You can buy emeralds in Colombia.

B. Now talk to your partner about the different stones and metals. What do you know about them?

Stone or Metal		Country
emeralds		
gold		Thailand
jade		
lapiz		Chile
opals		
pearls		Japan
silver		
turquoise		United States

Unit 24

1. Read this riddle to student A.

One day a girl went down a one-way street in the wrong direction. She didn't break the law. Why?

If your partner can't solve it, give this hint:
Is the law about walking or driving?
Answer to Student A's riddle: *The girl was walking.*

2. Student A will read this riddle. Try to solve it. Look at the picture to help you. If you can't solve it, say, "Can I have a hint?".

Tapescript

Unit 1 Actors

Page 2 Facts

A
1. Comedies are funny.
2. A director makes movies.
3. The main actor is the star.
4. Many movies are made in Hollywood.
5. Before a play, you say to an actor, "Break a leg." It means good luck.

Page 4 Listening Comprehension 1

Male: Are you trying out for the new play?
Female: Yes.
Male: Me, too. What part do you want?
Female: I want to be Jen.
Male: Jen? That's the biggest part.
Female: I know.
Male: Well, I'll be happy with any part . . . How did you hear about this play? Did you read the ad in *The Actor's Newspaper*?
Female: No, my dad told me about it.
Male: Oh? Does he work for the paper?
Female: No.
Male: Is he an actor?
Female: No. He's the director.
Male: Oh.

Page 4 Conversation Practice

1. A: What kind of movie is *The Mask of Zorro*?
   B: It's an action film.
2. A: What time is the next show?
   B: The next show is at 7:00 p.m.
3. A: Who's in it?
   B: Antonio Banderas.
4. A: Can I have two tickets, please?
   B: That'll be $14.00.

Page 5 Listening Comprehension 2

A: Is Banderas his real name?
B: His real name is Bandera, B-A-N-D-E-R-A, without the "s."
A: When and where was he born?
B: He was born in Malaga, Spain, on August 10, 1960.
A: Does he have any brothers and sisters?
B: He has one brother.
A: Is Banderas married?
B: Yes, he is. His wife is the actress Melanie Griffith.

Unit 2 Books

Page 6 Facts

A
1. You buy books at a bookstore.
2. A "bestseller" is a popular book.
3. There are paperback and hard cover books.
4. Agatha Christie's books sold over 2 billion copies.
5. A "whodunit" is a mystery.

Page 8 Listening Comprehension 1

Miki: Hi, I'm Miki Rice. Can I ask you some questions? I'm doing a school report.
Man 1: No problem.
Miki: Well, I see you're carrying a book. Where do you get your books?
Man 1: I buy them at a super bookstore. I love those stores.
Miki: Thanks. And you, sir? Where do you get your books?
Man 2: I buy them online.
Miki: Thank you . . . Uh, hi. I'm Miki Rice. I'm doing a school report. Where do you get your books?
Woman 1: Well, sometimes I buy them at a neighborhood store. And sometimes I borrow them from the library.
Miki: Thanks a lot. How about you?
Woman 2: I borrow them.
Miki: From the library?
Woman 2: No—from my friend. Megan, when will you finish that book?
Woman 1: Tomorrow.
Miki: Thank you both so much.
Woman 1: You're welcome. Good luck with your report.

Page 8 Conversation Practice

1. Salesperson: May I help you?
   Customer: Yes, thank you. I'm looking for a book about chocolate.
2. Salesperson: What's the name of the book?
   Customer: It's called, *Smart People Like Chocolate*.
3. Salesperson: Who's the author?
   Customer: It's by Coco Bean.
4. Salesperson: Let me check the computer . . . We have one copy. It's on that shelf.
   Customer: Thanks.

Page 9 Listening Comprehension 2

Harry Potter books are popular all over the world. You can find them in 200 countries. You can read them in fifty-five languages. The sales of the fifth Harry Potter book were great. Barnes & Noble bookstores expected to sell 1 million copies in the first week. The bookstores sold one million copies in the first forty-eight hours.

J.K. Rowling is the author of the Harry Potter books. Her first four books sold 192 million copies worldwide. Before she wrote Harry Potter, Rowling was poor. Today she is very rich. Why are her books so popular? Bookseller Ben Jones says, "They have something for everyone—a good story, a lot of action, and a fight in which the good guys win."

Unit 3 Chocolate

Page 10 Facts

A

1. The Maya made chocolate 1,700 years ago.
2. The Aztecs used cocoa beans for money.
3. The Aztecs put chilies in their chocolate drink.
4. The Spanish introduced chocolate to the rest of Europe.
5. The average American eats about twelve pounds of chocolate a year.

Page 12 Listening Comprehension 1

Man:	Here. Have some chocolate.
Woman:	No thanks.
Man:	Why not? It's good for you.
Woman:	It is? Says who?
Man:	Well, a scientific study showed that chocolate is good for the heart.
Woman:	Really? Who did the study?
Man:	Scientists in Germany.
Woman:	And what did it show?
Man:	Dark chocolate lowered blood pressure.
Woman:	What about white chocolate?
Man:	No, only dark chocolate.
Woman:	Hmm. That's interesting. Uh . . . How many people were in the study?
Man:	Thirteen.
Woman:	Only thirteen? *(laughs softly)*
Man:	Yeah. I guess it's better to have more people in a study.
Woman:	I guess so. I'll have an apple, please.

Page 12 Conversation Practice

1. A: Hi.
   B: Here, this is for you.
   A: Thanks.
2. A: OK if I open it?
   B: Sure. Go right ahead.
3. A: Thanks so much. I love chocolate.
   B: I'm glad.
4. A: Let's try some.
   B: OK. Let's.
5. A: Mmm. It's delicious.
   B: Mmm. You're right. It is good.

Page 13 Listening Comprehension 2

Chocolate makers have names for different kinds of chocolate. One kind of chocolate is called "ganache." We spell it g-a-n-a-c-h-e. It's a French word. Ganache is a mixture of chocolate and cream. This chocolate was first made in France in the 19th century.

A worker in a chocolate company was careless. He dropped cream in some chocolate. His boss was angry at him. He called him stupid. The French word for a stupid person is "ganache." But the chocolate with cream tasted delicious. Today all chocolate makers call smooth chocolate with cream in it "ganache."

Unit 4 Diamonds and Other Jewelry

Page 14 Facts

A

1. Until the mid-1700s, most diamonds came from India.
2. The biggest diamond in the world is the Star of Africa.
3. We measure diamonds in carats.
4. Most diamonds are about 3 billion years old.
5. Diamonds are the hardest stones.
6. Gold and silver are metals. Diamonds and emeralds are stones.

Page 16 Listening Comprehension 1

All over the world people judge diamonds in the same way. They use the four Cs. What are they? Can you guess? They are carat, clarity, color, and cut.

Many people think that carat means size. This isn't true. Carat is about weight. Clarity is what you see in a diamond. The best diamonds are the clearest. These diamonds are very hard to find. When you judge a diamond's color, you are really looking for no color. The most expensive diamonds have the least color.

Finally, cut is about the sides of the diamond. A good cut makes the diamond more beautiful. Today most diamonds are in engagement rings. How much money do people spend on an engagement ring? Some diamond salespeople say two months salary. But, of course, you should do whatever you feel comfortable with.

Page 16 Listening Comprehension 2

Bob:	Good afternoon, everyone. Today we have a tour guide who works at the Smithsonian Institute, a museum in Washington, D.C. She's here to tell us about the Hope Diamond. Welcome to our show. *(applause)*
TG:	Hi, Bob. Thanks.
Bob:	So tell us . . . Why is the Hope Diamond so famous?
TG:	Well, there are two reasons. First, it's big and beautiful. And second, the Hope Diamond has a very special history.
Bob:	What do you mean?
TG:	People say it has a curse.
Bob:	A curse?
TG:	Yes. They say the Hope Diamond brings bad luck to its owner.
Bob:	Is that true?
TG:	I don't know. But many of its owners had sad lives.
Bob:	Where did the diamond come from?
TG:	India.
Bob:	And can people see the diamond today?
TG:	Yes. Just go to the Smithsonian Institute in Washington, D.C. You can see it there.
Bob:	That's great. Thank you very much.

Unit 5 Emergencies and Disasters

Page 18 Facts

A

1. Something dangerous happens. You need to act now. You say, "This is an emergency."
2. You need to get to a hospital. You call an ambulance.
3. People in an accident are taken to the E.R. (emergency room) in a hospital.
4. The earth shakes during an earthquake.
5. Strong storms in the Atlantic Ocean or Caribbean Sea are called hurricanes.
6. Strong storms in the Pacific Ocean or Indian Ocean are called typhoons.

Page 20 Listening Comprehension 1

Marco: Hi, Karen? How're you doing?

Karen: Good. How are things in Mexico?

Marco: Great. I just read about the blackout in Ohio. Are you and Bob OK?

Karen: Oh, yes. I was at home. I was sending a fax when all the electricity went out. Bob was home, too.

Marco: That's good.

Karen: Bob said, "Karen, what did you do?" I said, "I don't know. I hope I didn't break the fax machine." Then we saw it was a blackout. The lights went out everywhere. I said, "Bob, you always say I break machines. This time it wasn't me." We laughed and he said he was sorry. Then we ate all the ice cream in the freezer. We ate in the dark.

Marco: Well, I'm just glad you're OK.

Karen: Thanks for calling.

Page 21 Listening Comprehension 2

There are thousands of forest fires in Canada every year. It's not surprising because there are a lot of forests in Canada. Canada spends millions of dollars fighting these fires.

The fires usually start in April with grass fires. Then in May or June the forest fires begin. By September, about 2,000 square kilometers burn with 9,500 fires across the country. During those six months Canada hires hundreds of firefighters. Some are trained firefighters. Others are college students who need a job. The government spends millions of dollars protecting the trees. And with good reason: Canada is a forest nation. It is the world's largest exporter of wood and paper.

More than half of the fires (58%) are caused by humans. The rest are caused by lightning. We know that as long as there is fire, there will be forest fires.

Unit 6 Fables and Fairy Tales

Page 22 Facts

A

1. Fables are stories about animals that talk.
2. Aesop's Fables are over 2,300 years old. Aesop was from Greece.
3. There are many kings, queens, princes, and princesses in fairy tales.
4. Fairy tales often begin, "Once upon a time . . ."
5. Fairy tales often end, "They lived happily ever after."
6. Hans Christian Andersen wrote *The Little Mermaid* and *The Ugly Duckling.*

Page 24 Listening Comprehension 1

Once upon a time there was a mother duck. She sat on her eggs waiting for them to hatch. Finally the babies were born. One was big and ugly. The other ducks made him feel bad. They told him he was big and ugly. He felt bad all winter long. But in the spring he began to change. He turned into a beautiful swan. He was very happy.

Some people say that this story is a lot like Andersen's own life. He was born very poor. Later he became rich, famous and successful. People weren't nice to him in his early life, but they treated him very well later on.

Page 24 Conversation Practice

Once upon a time, a miser sold all he had and bought a lump of gold. He buried the gold in a hole in the ground. Every day after that, he went to look at his gold. One of the miser's workmen watched the miser and saw the gold. The next night the workman stole the gold. When the miser found the hole empty, he began to shout and scream. A neighbor heard the story and said to the miser: "There's no need for you to shout and scream. Take a stone, and place it in the hole. Pretend it is the gold. After all, you never used the gold for anything."

Page 25 Listening Comprehension 2

One hot summer day, a fox was taking a walk. He saw a bunch of grapes. He wanted to eat the grapes, but the grapes were on a branch and they were hard to reach.

Twice the fox tried to reach the grapes. He couldn't reach them. Finally, he walked away with his nose in the air and said, "I'm sure those grapes are sour!"

Unit 7 Gestures

Page 26 Facts

A

1. Gestures are one kind of body language.
2. In Asia, a smile sometimes means you are embarrassed.
3. In most countries, moving your head up and down means "yes." But in Bulgaria, it means "no."
4. At plays, lectures, and concerts in Europe, some people whistle when they don't like something.
5. Business people in the United States shake hands firmly and look you in the eye.

Page 28 Listening Comprehension 1

There is one gesture that we all know. People almost always understand it. Little children and presidents use it. Scientists say that it is good for your health. It makes you feel good. Do you know what this gesture is? It begins with the letter "s." Now look at your classmates. How many are using this gesture now? Are you?

Page 29 Listening Comprehension 2

In Brazil, when people meet, they shake hands. The handshake often lasts a long time. People shake hands when they say "hello" and when they say "good-bye." It's important to look at the person when you shake hands. Also, it's important to shake the hand of everyone in a room.

In Brazil touching other people is OK. People touch other people's arms, elbows, and backs. Also, it's OK to interrupt during a conversation. It shows that you're interested.

Unit 8 Hairstyles

Page 30 Facts

A
1. The average head has 100,000 hairs.
2. The average person loses about 100 hairs a day.
3. Someone without hair is bald.
4. Hair grows faster in cold weather.
5. British judges wear wigs.

Page 32 Listening Comprehension 1

A: Hello, Renée's Hair Salon, can I help you?
B: Hello. This is Meg Lyons. I'd like to make an appointment with Nick for a cut and style for tomorrow, Thursday.
A: OK. What time can you come?
B: Is he free at eleven?
A: Let me check. No, sorry. He's busy then. How about one-thirty?
B: Uh, . . . How about one?
A: OK. Is that L-Y-O-N-S?
B: Yes, that's right.
A: Then I'll see you tomorrow.
B: Thanks a lot. Bye.
A: Bye.

Page 33 Listening Comprehension 2

Judges in Great Britain wear wigs. The custom began in the 1660s when all the rich people wore wigs. Judges' wigs are made of horsehair, and they're not comfortable. They're very heavy. And wigs that belonged to great judges can be very expensive. British judges receive money to buy their wigs, but lawyers in court must buy their own. Many people think wigs look funny.

Do judges ever complain about this custom? Do they want to change it? In the 1990s judges talked about getting rid of the wigs, but nothing happened and British judges today still wear wigs.

Unit 9 Ice

Page 34 Facts

A
1. Ice is the same weight as water.
2. The ice age started 3 million years ago and ended 11,000 years ago.
3. An iceberg is a large piece of ice moving in the ocean. Almost 90% of an iceberg is below water.
4. The native people of Northern Canada used to live in igloos.
5. When you meet people and say something that makes them feel comfortable, you are "breaking the ice."
6. When you want a drink with ice cubes, you ask for a drink "on the rocks."

Page 36 Listening Comprehension 1

Duncan Hamilton is an artist. He is a sculptor, but his work only lasts for a short time, usually for only six or seven hours. That's because Duncan is an ice sculptor. He began sculpting ice in the 1970s. Before that he worked as a chef at a top London restaurant. Today, Duncan has an international reputation. He does sculptures for weddings, parties, business events, and other special occasions. All his sculptures are original. He never works from a mold. According to Duncan, ice sculptures look best when they start to melt. Duncan says, "I think of the sculptures as a show. That's why I don't feel bad when they melt."

Page 37 Listening Comprehension 2

The word "Inuit" means "real people." It is the name for some of the native people of Canada. In April 1999 the Canadian government gave the Inuit land. The land is now called Nunavut. It is the newest and largest part of Canada. It is 20% of the country. Almost 26,000 people live there, and 85% of them are Inuit. Today most Inuit live in towns and houses. They don't live in igloos and they don't use dog sleds. They have refrigerators, stoves, TVs, and computers. And they travel by snowmobile in winter and plane in the summer.

But the Inuit follow some old traditions. The older people tell their stories in order to keep their old ideas alive. The family and nature are still important parts of their lives. And the Inuit continue to make beautiful sculptures of people and animals.

Unit 10 Junk and Garbage

Page 38 Facts

A
1. Soda, candy, and potato chips are examples of junk food.
2. Companies send mail we don't want. We call this mail junk mail. Americans throw away 44% of this mail without opening it.
3. E-mail ads are called spam.
4. A market with old or used things is a flea market.
5. People put things in front of their houses and sell them at a garage sale.
6. When you use something again, you recycle it.

Page 40 Listening Comprehension 1

In June 2003 people saw a bright light in the sky above Tasmania in Australia. Nobody knew where it came from. Some thought it was a shooting star, but others thought it was space junk.

Some scientists are worried about junk on earth. But other scientists are worried about junk in space. There is a lot of junk in space. Scientists know of 9,000 pieces of junk. There are three questions people ask: Is this junk dangerous for people on space missions? Is it dangerous for people on earth? Is there anything we can do about it?

Space junk hasn't hurt anyone yet. But it may hurt someone in the future. Scientists are keeping records of space junk. Scientists know what to do about it, but nobody wants to do anything because it would cost too much.

A few months after Janet was married, her grandmother gave her a lamp. Janet didn't like the lamp. One day she decided to throw it away. A week later she met a neighbor. Janet and the woman became friends. The woman invited Janet for dinner. When Janet came to her home, she saw her grandmother's lamp. Janet smiled, but she didn't say anything to her new friend. Several months later she went to a store. She saw the same lamp. It was very expensive. She discovered her grandmother's lamp was an antique.

Unit 11 Kandinsky, Klee, and Modern Art

Page 42 Facts

A

1. Kandinsky was one of the first abstract artists.
2. Klee's paintings are not big and bold.
3. Paul Klee was born in Switzerland in 1879.
4. Wassily Kandinsky was born in Moscow in 1866.
5. Before he became an artist, Kandinsky studied law at the University of Moscow.
6. Klee and Kandinsky were friends.

Page 44 Listening Comprehension 1

Kandinsky and Klee were important European artists. They were alike in many ways. They had many talents. Both men came from musical families and music was an important part of their lives. Both men worked at the Bauhaus school in Germany. They met and became good friends. Both men wrote about their art. And both men today are important to the history of modern art.

Page 44 Listening Comprehension 2

Art is all around us. Artists have a part in buildings, furniture, books, and clothes. Some art is easy to understand. Some art is hard to understand. Here are some questions that can help you understand art:

First of all, how is this art like other art?

Next, what do you know about the artist?

Third, when and where was this art made?

Fourth, does it tell a story? Does it tell about a person, a place, or an event?

Fifth, does this art make you feel or remember anything? For example, does it make you feel happy, angry, sad, or frightened? Do you think that the artist felt the same way?

Finally, what is this art made of? Are the materials important to the idea behind the art?

Unit 12 Laughter

Page 46 Facts

A

1. The average person laughs thirteen times a day.
2. Both chimpanzees and baby rats laugh.
3. A baby begins to laugh at four months.
4. "Laughter is the best medicine" is a famous saying.
5. When you are not serious about something, you say, "I'm just kidding."
6. When you "get" a joke, you understand it.

Page 48 Listening Comprehension 1

"That was a funny movie. I laughed so hard I cried!"

Why do we laugh? Experts say there are three explanations. First of all, we laugh when there is a surprise. We expect one thing to happen, but something else happens. For example, a teenager is on the telephone for thirty minutes. Her father says, "That was short. You usually talk for two hours." The girl replies, "It was a wrong number."

Second, we laugh at someone's mistake. We laugh because we feel we are better or smarter. That is why people laugh when someone slips on a banana peel or when someone says something stupid.

Third, we laugh when we feel relief from stress. We see this a lot in movies. The tension in a movie increases. We are very nervous. Suddenly someone says or does something funny. We feel relief and laugh.

Page 48 Conversation Practice

Once there was a mother cat and three baby kittens. The mother cat said to her kittens, "It's a beautiful day. Go take a walk." The kittens walked for a while when they saw a dog. The dog looked at the baby kittens and barked, "Woof, woof." The kittens ran back home. Their mother said, "Why are you here?" The kittens replied, "Meow, meow. There was a big dog. He barked at us and scared us." The mother cat said, "Come with me." So the mother cat and the kittens started to walk. Again the dog appeared and barked at the four cats. Now the mother cat smiled at her kittens and said, "Watch me." Then she looked the dog in his eyes and said, "Woof, woof." The dog walked away. The cat turned to her kittens and said, "Now you see the importance of a second language!"

Page 49 Listening Comprehension 2

Almost everyone says it's good to laugh. Scientists say it's good for your health, and it makes you feel good. They say laughter is like exercise. Both laughter and exercise lower blood pressure. They make your blood move faster and they use different muscles in the body.

Here are two ways you can put more laughter in your life: First of all, decide what makes you laugh. Then, meet with people who make you laugh.

Unit 13 Masks

Page 50 Facts

A

1. Both Brazil and Venice have celebrations with masks and costumes.
2. Children in Canada and the United States wear costumes and masks on Halloween.
3. *Noh* theater started in Japan in the 14th century. In *Noh* plays, the main actors wear masks. All the actors are men.
4. On the Chinese New Year people wear masks and costumes and do a lion dance.
5. A lawyer does not wear a mask.

Page 52 Listening Comprehension 1

For one week every February people go to Venice to see the Venice Carnival. At the Carnival everyone wears a mask. This modern Carnival began in the 1980s. But masks are not new to Venice.

Two hundred years ago Venetians, the people who lived in Venice, wore masks all the time. It was the custom. Many Venetians were rich and powerful. Some of them started to wear masks because they didn't want others to know their business. But then things changed in Venice. People became dishonest and they used the masks to help them commit crimes. So new laws arose. People could only wear masks at certain hours of the day. By the end of the 18th century the Venetian Republic ended, and so did the custom of wearing masks.

Page 53 Listening Comprehension 2

This is an animal mask. It's from Burkino Faso, a country in Africa. It's worn by the Nuna people. It's made of wood. The animal masks of the Nuna people all have large eyes and short three-sided noses.

Dancers wear these masks on market day and when someone dies. People sing and play drums while the dancers dance.

Unit 14 Names, Nicknames, and Titles

Page 54 Facts

A
1. We use the title Ms. before a married or unmarried woman's name.
2. In North America, a person's family name is his or her last name.
3. The initials of Johann Sebastian Bach are JSB.
4. A professor teaches at a university.
5. Some writers give themselves pen names.
6. In Canada and the United States, it's incorrect to call a teacher "Teacher." We call a teacher by his or her name.

Page 56 Listening Comprehension 1

Mike: Good afternoon. I'm Mike Jones and welcome to *The Name Game*. Our first player is Ashley Jones. Ashley, could you tell us something about yourself?
Ashley: Sure, Mike. I'm a teacher from Seattle, Washington.
Mike: OK. Now are you ready?
Ashley: Yes, I am.
Mike: Well then, Ashley. Here's the first question.
            Who had the initials JFK and who was this person?
Ashley: John Fitzgerald Kennedy. He was a President of the United States.
Mike: Right you are.
            Our second question . . .
            Do you know the pen name for Samuel Clemens?
            Samuel Clemens wrote the book *Huckleberry Finn*.
Ashley: Mark Twain.
Mike: Great. Our third question . . . This musician's real name is Richard Starkey. What's his stage name?
Ashley: Ringo Starr, one of the Beatles.
Mike: You're right again. Congratulations! You have just won $3,000!
Ashley: Thank you, Mike.
Mike: You're welcome. That's all folks. Good night.

Page 56 Listening Comprehension 2

German citizens cannot give their children any name they want. When a baby is born, the parents may choose the name, but the government decides if it's OK. This rule is over 130 years old. The government doesn't want a name that makes a child feel bad. The name must not be too strange. Boys' names must be different from girls' names. So, what happens if the government doesn't like a name? The parents can go to court. Then a judge decides.

Unit 15 Ounces and Other Measurments

Page 58 Facts

A
1. The short form of *ounce* is *oz*. The short form of *pound* is *lb*.
2. Most of the world uses the metric system. Only the United States, Myanmar, and Liberia don't use it.
3. The metric system was created by French scientists in the 18th century.
4. A meter is a little more than one yard.
5. A liter is a little less than a quart.

Page 60 Listening Comprehension 1

A prefix is a group of letters at the beginning of a word. Some prefixes tell you a number. For example, "bi-, b-i" means "two." A bicycle has two wheels and a bilingual person speaks two languages. Some prefixes help you understand measures. For example, the prefix "centi-, c-e-n-t-i" means "one one-hundredth." One centimeter is one one-hundredth of a meter. The prefix "kilo-, k-i-l-o" means "one thousand." One kilometer is one thousand meters, and one kilogram is one thousand grams.

Page 61 Listening Comprehension 2

Oscar: I'm Oscar Mann. Welcome to *Ask Any Question*. Today's show is about measurements. And here's our first caller.
First caller : Hi, Oscar. Can you answer this question? Sometimes "meter" is spelled "m-e-t-e-r" and sometimes it's spelled "m-e-t-r-e." Sometimes "liter" is spelled "l-i-t-e-r" and sometimes it's spelled "l-i-t-r-e." What's the difference?
Oscar: There's no difference. The British use the "r-e" spelling and the Americans use the "e-r" spelling.
First caller: Thanks, Oscar.
Oscar: And here's our next caller.
2nd caller: Hello, Oscar. I'd like to know why the short form of "pound" is "l-b."
Oscar: That's a good question. It comes from the Romans. Many years ago, the Romans came to Britain. They used the word "libra" for a weight. The British called it a pound but they kept the short form "l-b" from the word "libra."
2nd caller: Thank you.
Oscar: We have time for one more question.
3rd caller: Someone told me that the "hand" is a measurement. Is that true?
Oscar: Well, it used to be, but now it isn't except in one case. We use the "hand" to measure the height of a horse. One hand is a little more than ten centimeters or four inches.
3rd caller: Thank you, Oscar.
Oscar: And thank you ladies and gentlemen for listening to *Ask Any Question*.

Unit 16 Photography

Page 62 Facts

A

1. English-speaking photographers often say, "Say cheese."
2. A *snapshot* is a photo.
3. You need a flash to take pictures in the dark.
4. A portrait is a picture of a person.
5. A landscape is a picture of nature.
6. People keep family photos in a photo album.

Page 64 Listening Comprehension 1

Alfred Steiglitz was born in Hoboken, New Jersey, in 1864. His parents were German and he studied in both Berlin and New York. He bought his first camera in Berlin at the age of nineteen. That's when photography became his life's work.

He always wanted to show that photography was for everyone. He often worked with people who had simple cameras and little training. He loved to take photos in the rain, in the fog, and in the darkness.

Steiglitz opened a gallery of "art" photographers in 1905 on Fifth Avenue in New York. There, people saw the works of photographers and modern artists, too. One of the modern artists with paintings in the gallery, was Georgia O'Keefe. Steiglitz and O'Keefe fell in love. In 1918 Steiglitz left his first wife and married Georgia O'Keefe. They were often apart, but remained married until he died at eighty-two.

Page 65 Listening Comprehension 2

A: Hey, Jack, is that your family?
B: Uh-huh. We were at Amoré Restaurant for my grandma's birthday.
A: Is that an Italian restaurant?
B: Yes. It's my grandma's favorite. We go there at least once a month.
A: I didn't know you had a sister.
B: Yeah, that's Carmen. She's into dance. She dances for hours every day.
A: I'll bet she's good.
B: I guess so.
A: That pasta looks delicious.
B: Everything at Amoré is delicious. I'll take you there on your next birthday. When is it?
A: Tomorrow.
B: Really?
A: No. It's in January.

Unit 17 Queens

Page 66 Facts

A

1. Queen Victoria of England was queen for sixty-four years, from 1837 to 1901.
2. Cleopatra VII was the last queen of Egypt. She ruled from 69 to 30 BCE.
3. The Queen of Sheba was married to King Solomon.
4. Hawaii is the only state in the United States that had kings and queens.
5. The queen bee is the most important one in the family.
6. The queen is the most powerful piece in a chess game.

Page 68 Listening Comprehension 1

In the past only one U.S. state was ruled by kings and queens. It was Hawaii. Hawaii was a monarchy for eighty-three years. The last monarch to rule was Queen Liliuokalani. She was queen from 1891 to 1893. In 1893 she was forced to give up her throne to the United States.

The Hawaiian people liked her a lot. She was a woman of courage and creativity. She loved the Hawaiian people and tried to help them. Queen Liliuokalani was also a talented composer. She wrote more than 165 songs including "Aloha Oe." That song is probably the best know Hawaiian song ever. She lived from 1838 to 1917. Today you can see her statue on the grounds of the state capitol in Honolulu.

Page 69 Listening Comprehension 2

Come take a trip on the luxurious *Queen Mary 2*. It is the largest, longest, tallest, and most expensive ship ever. It has something for everyone. There are 5 swimming pools, 10 restaurants, shops, and a super luxury spa. There's even a planetarium. And you can bring the children. British nannies will watch them. So for the vacation of a lifetime, take a cruise on the *Queen Mary 2*.

Unit 18 "Red" Idioms

Page 70 Facts

A

1. She *saw red* when he asked for more money. She was angry.
2. Her jewelry was in his pocket. They caught him *red-handed*. He was doing something illegal.
3. He took the *red-eye* from San Francisco to New York. He took a night flight.
4. The company is *in the red*. The company is not doing well.
5. The Yankees were *red hot* last night. They won the game 11–0.

Page 72 Listening Comprehension 1

When we have a lot of paperwork, we say we have a lot of "red tape." The expression "red tape" began in England in the 18th century. At that time, lawyers and government officials held their papers together with tape that was red. When someone spoke about "cutting through red tape," they meant it. By the 19th century, lawyers stopped using red tape, but the expression "red tape" was still used to mean unnecessary paperwork.

Page 72 Listening Comprehension 2

Different colors make people feel and act in different ways. Here is some information about the colors red and blue.

Scientists say red raises blood pressure. It also makes a person breathe faster. Red makes people look—it grabs their attention. Sometimes red makes people feel like fighting.

Blue is very different. Blue relaxes people. That's why many people paint their bedrooms blue. Sometimes blue makes people feel sad. Scientists say people work harder in a blue room and weight-lifters lift heavier weights in blue gyms.

Unit 19 Strange and Unusual Things

Page 74 Facts

A

1. It's impossible for people to lick their elbows.
2. Women blink nearly twice as often as men.
3. More people use blue toothbrushes than red ones.
4. A cockroach can live several weeks with its head cut off.
5. You're born with about 300 bones. When you are an adult you have 206 bones.
6. You want to say something surprising. You begin, "Believe it or not."

Page 76 Listening Comprehension 1

In Tennessee, it is against the law to drive a car while sleeping.

In Virginia, chickens cannot lay eggs before 8:00 a.m. and must be done before 4:00 p.m.

In Cleveland, Ohio, it is unlawful to leave chewing gum in public places.

In Missouri, a man must have a permit to shave.

In Massachusetts, it is against the law to put tomatoes in clam chowder.

In North Carolina, it is against the law for a rabbit to race down the street.

In Corpus Christie, Texas, it is illegal to raise alligators in your home.

Page 77 Listening Comprehension 2

Long necks are a sign of beauty in Myanmar. Women put large copper rings around their necks. This makes their necks longer. The longest neck on record is 40 cm (15.75 in.).

Hoo Sateow lives in India. When he was 18, he got a haircut. Soon after, he got sick. He never cut his hair again. His hair is now 5.15 meters long (16 ft. ll in.).

Unit 20 Tai Chi and Other Martial Arts

Page 78 Facts

A

1. Tai chi helps both the mind and body.
2. Judo comes from Japan. It means "empty hand."
3. Tae kwon do comes from Korea. It is famous for high kicks.
4. Moves of the tiger, crane, leopard, snake, and dragon are a part of kung fu.
5. The first judo competition at the Olympic Games was in 1964.

Page 80 Listening Comprehension 1

Learn to relax and feel good. Join our tai chi classes. They will begin the last Monday in January. They're open to all students and their families. Classes will be held from 6:30 to 7:20 in the morning every Monday, Wednesday, and Friday. We will meet in West Park near the soccer field. For more information call (881) 555–0908.

Page 81 Listening Comprehension 2

Man: Hello. Bill Pace speaking.
Amy: Hello, I'm Amy Lam. I heard the ad on the radio for tai chi classes. I'd like to take the classes. I just have a few questions.
Man: OK. I'll try and answer them.

Amy: First of all, do I need special clothes?
Man: No, you don't. Loose clothes are best. You need to move freely.
Amy: What about on my feet? Do I need special shoes?
Man: No, but you can't wear heels. Light footwear is important. The Chinese slipper called the kung fu shoe is best.
Amy: Do people use tai chi to attack in self-defense?
Man: Yes, they do.
Amy: Why is tai chi so popular today?
Man: I think it's because it helps people relax. And almost anyone can do it—men and women, young and old.

Unit 21 Uncles

Page 82 Facts

A

1. Your great-uncle is a brother of your grandmother or grandfather
2. The U.S. government is sometimes called Uncle Sam.
3. Your uncle's wife is your aunt.
4. *Uncle Tom's Cabin* is a book by Harriet Beecher Stowe.
5. You say "I'll be a monkey's uncle" when you are surprised to hear something.

Page 84 Listening Comprehension 1

My mother has two brothers and one sister. My mother's sister is married. Her brothers are single. My father has one brother and three sisters. Two of my father's sisters are married. One is single.

Page 85 Listening Comprehension 2

"I'll be a monkey's uncle" was first used in the 19th century. Charles Darwin, a British scientist, wrote a book called *Descent of Man*. In his book he said that humans, apes, and monkeys all had the same ancestors. Some people didn't like this idea. His idea surprised people. They were the first ones to say—"I'll be a monkey's uncle." Today the expression means—"I'm surprised to hear that!"

Unit 22 Vending Machines

Page 86 Facts

A

1. In 1880 in England, the first vending machine sold postcards.
2. For over sixty years, Horn and Hardart was a cafeteria chain in the United States. The food was behind glass doors. To get the food, you put money in an opening. The restaurant opened in 1902.
3. You need exact change for some vending machines.
4. Vending machines have an opening for coins. The opening is called a slot.
5. Japan has the largest variety of vending machines.

Page 88 Listening Comprehension 1

Today you can buy all sorts of things from vending machines. An online site reported the following:

- In France there is a vending machine for blue jeans. The machine has a belt for you to measure your waist.
- In the U.S. and Canada you can buy live shrimp, frogs, and worms from vending machines. These machines are for fishermen.

- In Japan vending machines near temples sell fortunes, like the kind you see in fortune cookies.
- During an art festival in Sweden there was a vending machine nearby. It sold paintings by famous artists.

Page 88 Listening Comprehension 2

Kim Won Jung walked up to a vending machine. She bought an orange drink. She didn't use coins. She used her cell phone to pay for her drink.

In South Korea today the cell phone is for more than talking. Telecom companies are working together with credit card companies and banks. People pay for everything from groceries to gasoline using their cell phones.

In South Korea today there are 33.2 million cell phone users. The country has 48 million people. People use cell phones to surf the Internet, transfer money, play the lottery, buy movie tickets, and take pictures.

Unit 23 Weddings

Page 90 Facts

A

1. In a traditional Western wedding, the bride wears a white wedding gown.
2. The man getting married is called the groom.
3. You think two people will marry. You say, "I hear wedding bells."
4. At traditional weddings in Mexico, the groom gives his bride thirteen gold coins.
5. At traditional weddings in India, someone paints the bride's hands.
6. After a wedding, the couple often goes on a honeymoon.

Page 92 Listening Comprehension 1

Carmen: Hi, Pranee. Welcome back. How was Thailand and how was your sister's wedding?
Pranee: Great. Here. I have photos of the wedding.
Carmen: Oh. Your sister looks beautiful.
Pranee: Thank you.
Carmen: Is that you?
Pranee: Yes, it is. I'm with my younger brother and my parents.
Carmen: You all look wonderful. What are the people doing in that photo?
Pranee: This is a Thai wedding custom. It's called Khan Mark.
Carmen: Who are all the people?
Pranee: They're friends and relatives of the groom. They're visiting my parents' home. They must bring gold or silver for the bride and groom before they can pass the gate.
Carmen: That's good for the new couple.
Pranee: Yes. Marriage is a very big event in Thailand.

Page 93 Listening Comprehension 2

Gail: Hello.
Ming: Hi, Gail. It's Ming. Listen. I'm having a shower for Wendy.
Gail: That's great. When is it?
Ming: It's on March 21 in the afternoon.
Gail: Where?
Ming: At the Blue Bay Restaurant.
Gail: That's good. I'm free then. And the Blue Bay is a beautiful restaurant.

Ming: I'm so happy you can come. We're all bringing a recipe. a gift for the kitchen.
Gail: Good idea. I can get her a soup pot. And I'll give her my recipe for vegetable soup. It's easy and it tastes delicious.
Ming: Great. See you there. Bye.

Unit 24 X+Y=?

Page 94 Facts

A

1. A riddle is a question with a funny answer.
2. Someone finds the answer to a problem. The person says, "I've got it."
3. Some people can think of new ways to do things. We say they think "outside the box."
4. A picture with many pieces is a jigsaw puzzle.
5. In a crossword puzzle you try to find the correct word.

Page 96 Listening Comprehension 1

1. A: Why did the frog eat the lamp?
   B: I don't know. I give up.
   A: He wanted a light meal.
2. A: What side of a rabbit has the most fur?
   B: I don't know.
   A: The outside.
3. A: How far can you walk into a forest?
   B: Halfway. Then you're walking *out* of the forest.

Page 97 Listening Comprehension 2

Jam is heavier than Jelly.
Copper weighs more than Brandy, but less than Pumpkin.
Brandy weighs more than Jelly. Pumpkin weighs less than Jam.

Unit 25 Yen, Peso, and Other Currencies

Page 98 Facts

A

1. A U.S. dollar bill is 75% cotton.
2. "Can you change a dollar?" means you want coins for the dollar.
3. You have some yen. You want dollars. You ask, "What's the rate of exchange?"
4. Many countries in Europe use the euro.
5. The first person to collect coins was Augustus Caesar.
6. In the past people used cattle, tea, and shells as money.

Page 100 Listening Comprehension 1

Man: Excuse me, where can I change money?
Woman: There's a place on the second floor, across from the Information booth.
Man: Thanks.
(man at booth)
Woman: Hello.
Man: Can you help me? I'd like to change 10,000 yen into dollars.
Woman: Of course . . . Here you go. And here's your receipt.
Man: Thank you.

Welcome to the "Money Show." Good afternoon, Mr. Silver. I understand you are a coin collector.

Yes, I am. I started back in 1975. I find coins very exciting.

Bill: That's great. I have some questions for you. First of all, could you tell us . . . is an old coin more valuable than a newer coin?

Mr. Silver: Not always. You can buy a 600-year-old Roman coin for ten dollars. Some 1909 U.S. dimes are worth hundreds of dollars.

Bill: Hmm. That's good to know. Next, what do you think is most important in a coin?

Mr. Silver: You know when you buy a house, people say that location is most important. When you buy a coin, it's the condition of the coin. When it is hard to see the picture or read the writing on a coin, the coin is not worth much. So, a coin is best when it is like new. We call this "mint" condition.

Bill: Thank you, Mr. Silver. Our final question is about the care of coins. If you have dirty coins, is it a good idea to clean them?

Mr. Silver: Absolutely not. Never clean a coin. You can hurt it.

Bill: Thank you, Mr. Silver. I'm afraid our time is up. Thanks so much for coming today.

Mr. Silver: You're very welcome.

Unit 26 Zoos

Page 102 Facts

A

1. More than 4,500 years ago, there were zoos in Egypt.
2. The first zoos were built for kings and queens.
3. Today, the largest zoo in the world is in Berlin.
4. Most zoos today don't keep animals in cages.
5. An animal doctor is called a veterinarian.
6. Virginia McKenna was the star of a movie about animals called *Born Free*.

Page 104 Listening Comprehension 1

Zoos are very old. The first zoo was built in Egypt more than 4,500 years ago. But zoos then were different from zoos today. Early zoos were for kings and queens. Then later, zoos opened for all rich people. These zoos were built for the fun of the rich.

In China around 3,000 years ago an emperor created a very big zoo. It was more than 1,500 acres. He gave the zoo an interesting name. He called it the Garden of Intelligence.

Ancient Greeks built zoos, too. They built them in order to study animal and plant life. Students in Greece had to visit the zoos as part of their education.

From the 1400s to the 1700s new animals were brought to Europe from different parts of the world. The first public zoo opened in Austria in the 18th century. Soon, other countries followed. All the animals were kept in cages.

Today zoos are different. Animals aren't kept in cages. They can move around, just like in nature. There is an open feeling for the animals and the visitors.

But some people still think zoos are not good for animals. These people believe animals should be free. What do you think?

Page 104 Listening Comprehension 2

There are over 1,500 zoos in the world. The largest zoo is in Berlin, Germany. The Berlin Zoo has 13,000 animals. The Bronx Zoo in New York City is the second largest zoo. It has 6,000 animals.

The oldest public zoo is the Vienna Zoo, in Austria. It opened in 1752. The second oldest zoo is the London Zoo, which opened in 1828. At first it was used for scientific study. In 1847 it opened to the public. This was the first zoo to have a special children's zoo.